WHAT DO
WE DO NOW?

KEITH AND THE GIRL'S

WHAT DO
WE DO NOW?

SMART ANSWERS TO YOUR STUPID RELATIONSHIP QUESTIONS

 THREE RIVERS PRESS • NEW YORK

Published in the United States by Three Rivers Press, an imprint
of the Crown Publishing Group, a division of Random House, Inc.,
New York.

www.crownpublishing.com

Three Rivers Press and the Tugboat design are registered trade-
marks of Random House, Inc.

Library of Congress Cataloging-in-Publication Data
Malley, Keith.
     What do we do now? : Keith and The Girl's smart answers to
your stupid relationship questions / Keith Malley and Chemda
[Khalili].—1st ed.
     1. Man-woman relationships.   2. Dating (Social customs).
3. Couples.   I. Khalili, Chemda.   II. Title.
     HQ801.M3667 2010
     306.7—dc22

                                              2009047688

ISBN 978-0-307-45439-3

Printed in the United States of America

Design by Maria Elias

10 9 8 7 6 5 4 3 2 1

First Edition

This book is dedicated to all the listeners and supporters of the Keith and The Girl show. You have made KATG the juggernaut it has become, and we're very excited to present this book in your name.

Contents

A WARM WELCOME FROM THE EDITORS

The Keith and The Girl talk show has become one of the most popular and most downloaded comedy podcasts on the Internet by discussing life, pop culture, and, most notably for purposes of this book, relationships. Keith and Chemda utilize the unrestricted freedom that broadcasting over the Web gives them to do a show that is exactly what they want it to be: raw, funny, unique, totally unfiltered, and, most important, honest. When they talk about relationships, they talk about the problems, the hassles, the headaches, and every other way they can utterly and completely suck. They then offer their own brand of advice for listeners to fix all of these problems. Because if their relationship can work, then anybody's can.

 What the fuck does that mean: "If *their* relationship can work . . ."?

No, we just meant that you two are always around each other. You live together, began your own company together, work together, and continue to grow your business by leaps and bounds: live audience shows around the world; you do stand-up comedy; Chemda's a singer-songwriter; now you're authors. . . . What we meant to say was, considering how much time you spend with each other, it's amazing you can make it work. It's really a compliment.

Seemed a little negative, that's all.

Not at all. You keep a relationship going while managing your talk show and its following. Not bound by the rules of terrestrial or satellite radio, you guys openly say whatever you want five days a week. You'd think there'd be some things misspoken that would cause you two to want to kill each other, but you're both only sticking together better. I think you both are just terrific, and I know your hordes of fans and the media do as well.

Okay, okay. It's our first book is all. Maybe I'm a little nervous.

No reason to be.

Dear Reader, in *What Do We Do Now?*, Keith and Chemda are going to take the same approach that has made their show what it is (entirely one-of-a-kind) and apply it to a relationship book that actually lives up to the promise of being unique. They'll take all the misconceptions about life and love and unflinchingly sit you down and spell it out.

We'll literally spell it out. In words.

There are thousands of books on relationships—

Why would you tell them that? How about there *aren't* any other relationship books?

No, I'm saying that these other books all have the same dopey advice. These books are cherry-flavored bullshit. If all these copycat guides are so brilliant, why are not only divorces and the amount of broken homes skyrocketing, but the married authors themselves separating?

John Gray much? Snap.

Oh, shit, snap.

Hey, baby! When'd you get here?

They just edited me in, I guess.

As I was saying, this is where Keith and The Girl come in. From marriage to exes to fidelity, they will cover every thought-provoking question about relationships sent in by their audience. They share personal stories about every chapter topic—what they had to deal with and how they not only survived but prospered. You can jump from topic to topic (money, sex, affairs), question to question, or you can read from beginning to end. Sometimes Chemda and Keith agree completely on the answer; sometimes their styles, though they're on the same page, differ a little, and you can pick whose advice works better for your personality and exact situation. You'll learn things such as: A man isn't always supposed to buy flowers when a woman is angry, and a woman isn't always supposed to be coy when she's interested in a guy. This book doesn't give Band-Aids to the everyday relationship problems. It gives you the answers and cures the poisons that every couple faces. Whether you're looking to fix a new relationship or a long-standing relationship, or even to avoid the pitfalls of dating and spot the early warning signs, this book is for you.

Wait, what if people are homosexual? Is this book for gay people, too?

Our market research shows that gays don't read.

 Well they should, because it all still applies.

 Alright, baby. I'm ready if you're ready.

 In three ... two ...

Sex and Kink

We recently found out that wealthy people are buying other human beings and keeping them as pets. That is to say that they are petting, feeding, and disciplining them as if they were a dog or cat. This bothers me for a couple of reasons. One is that clearly the rich have run out of ideas on how to spend their money and I should quit this job and start an agency helping people spend their cash for a small fee. The second thing that annoys me is that this is yet another thing that was left out by my guidance counselor on the list of things I can be when I grow up. Not that I want to be a pet, but it makes me think, what else did that woman not offer that could have really been my calling?

This human pet thing, to me, seems like just another way certain people are choosing to express affection with one another. I can just see the "pets" at the end of the day masturbating about what a good job they did and how many treats they received. I am only partially judging. After all, kink is very natural. When it comes to kinky sex, generally, people tend to psychoanalyze others when hearing that their sexcapades are different from their own. It almost doesn't matter how crazy your sex is, chances are you will be making a face about someone else's practices. For me, sex is great when I'm being choked and ridiculed, but I think nipple clamps are for the crazy. But my preferences don't matter as long as Keith has a similar point of view. That's another reason why I think it's crazy when people want to wait until they're married to have sex. What if you find out that the person you just signed your life to can only get off if he wears your wedding gown because it makes him feel safe remembering that at one point in his life you were innocent?

It's incredible what people need in order to sustain what they call a life. For me, one of those things is sex. People who don't share my belief cannot be my friend. Seriously. I tried with these no-sex-having creeps. They don't get it. Also, they need to sit at the kids' table at dinner.

Sex is one of the only ways to increase and decrease your energy at the same time. It's magical. Plus it's the only real cure for a headache. Fuck or die.

And to you virgins: Quit trying to save it for anything special after the age of twenty-five. Good God, man. You're an adult now. Hurry up and get the disappointment out of the way so you can live your life. You only end up more fucked up and socially awkward the longer you wait. "What if I don't like it? What if I embarrass myself?" What if? There is no what if. You will. But the longer you wait, the more you're not going to be able to interact with people normally, and you're going to develop a whole series of anxieties. This is documented. Yes, documented right here because I had this published, but I bet it's documented in serious medical journals. We're the freaks because we like to choke and humiliate? No, you're the freak because you drip pre-cum in your sleep. FREAK! WEIRDO! FREAK!

I don't let virgins older than twenty-five in my house by

themselves. I don't trust them. There's something very strange about these people.

It's segments like this one in this book that are seriously going to have me disowned from my Catholic parents, but this is what I'm willing to do for you, dear reader. Get your shit together and open some legs.

If you're reading this in the bookstore, buy the book and bring it to the next book signing. We'll get you taken care of.

SEX AND KINK Questions

On the third date with this chick I've been dating, I slept with her. She's really cool, but it was the worst sexual experience of my life. Is this worth pursuing?

Wow, the worst in your whole life. I could see if the roles were reversed, and the girl was the one complaining. Maybe the guy was thrusting too hard, or he came too fast. But a guy complaining . . . don't get me wrong, girls can be lazy or just not have rhythm, but for it to be the worst . . . I say dump her. Or maybe throw her a bone a second time to be sure. Then dump her. If the roles were reversed, that's different, because, in general, a man has to really bring their game and a woman can just go with the flow. Sure, there are women who give it their all and surpass most other women, but for the most part it's hard for them to blow it. A guy, though, could be very excited or nervous. When a woman gets excited or nervous, her pussy doesn't go limp or squirt out her final load of the day. What the fuck was she doing? Twisting your dick and crying?

Wow, the *worst?*

The first time that Keith and I slept with each other, not only was the sex bad, but the kissing was horrendous too. I decided to see him again because I was really attracted to him and his personality, and I thought I'd give it another go because I enjoyed his company so much. We talked about how our kissing was not meshing, and it turned out that we were both trying so hard to please the other person that we were making up what we thought they wanted in our heads. Since our talk, the kissing automatically improved, and now he's my all-time favorite kisser. As for the sex, I always think that the first time isn't necessarily the best gauge on how a person is in bed. The sex can be awkward and uncomfortable when people are nervous and overexcited. Or, the sex can be unusually good (and not replicable) for people who lose their inhibitions when they don't know their partner.

You already slept with the girl. Why not try it a couple more times? Maybe be a little encouraging during the act. Throw her on top and see what happens. Maybe you both will learn something from the experience.

I just broke up with my girlfriend of one and a half years. She cheated on me, and now her best friend is hitting on me. Is revenge okay in this instance?

Definitely.

I'm having a hard time telling you not to do it. I thought of saying something like it's not going to make you feel as good as you anticipate, but it probably will. I thought of telling you that this would just show your ex that you're bitter. Who cares? You just fucked her best friend. And why shouldn't you be bitter about someone cheating on you? What can I say? I'm with Keith. Throw the best friend one and make sure it's the best she's ever gotten so that she can't help but tell the tale.

I've never had a one-night stand but have been wanting to try it. Is there any way to do that and not be called a slut?

Isn't the whole point to *be* called a slut?

Slut is just a term. Who's calling you a slut anyway? The guy whom you just slept with? I think he'll be busy feeling "lucky" and not worrying about your status as a female.

An important thing to keep in mind with the one-night stand (as a woman) is that you don't want to jump into it with just any half-decent guy who hits on you. Don't just do it for the opportunity to say that you've had a one-night stand. Do it for the experience. There's a big difference between an awful, regretful sexual incident and the fun you have building energy between you and a man you've never met. It's a much better experience when a natural heat develops between two people as opposed to just tickling an urge.

My point is that if you're going to go for it, start thinking of the word *slut* as not just a term, but rather a great story you'll never forget (to tell your girlfriends).

Good girl, Chemda. Keep preaching to girls that the word *slut* is positive. It gives my friends a better chance to bang these whores.

I want my girlfriend to go on the pill. How should I say it?

First, I'll tell you how *not* to say it. Don't act like you have the one penis that doesn't fit into any condom. Don't talk about how you can't feel anything and that she's lucky she doesn't have to wear one. Don't talk about it ruining the moment. That just makes women feel like you're making excuses. It also makes us feel like you haven't used condoms enough to learn which kind work for you and how to put them on with more finesse than a sixteen-year-old.

Instead, tell her that, since you are in an exclusive relationship, you were hoping that she would be willing to get on the pill. Include that you both will go to the doctor and get tested for STDs. This will show her that she's not as alone in the process and will reassure her that she's not putting herself at unknown risk.

How should you say it? I think you should say it with some nouns and a verb, and have at least one of those nouns be the object of the sentence. For example, you might say, "Hey honey, what do you think about going on the pill?" And then give her time to answer.

Look, she knows you're fucking her. I assume she knows, anyway. She does know, right? I think I have to call the police now if she doesn't know. Let's avoid the paperwork over here and say that she knows you plow her. It shouldn't be so crazy to ask her if she wants to take a pill that women have been taking for oh so many years. (That's how I wrote reports in high school. "Abraham Lincoln was our president oh so many years ago.")

If she's opposed because she thinks it's a sin or opposed because the pill messes with her body chemistry, get a pack of pills yourself and eat one every day as you say, "Mmmm, these are sooo delicious." You may be thinking your lady isn't a child and that this won't work, but she's fucking you regularly and won't go on the pill. She's either childish or retarded. However, I wouldn't use these adjectives in your initial sentence. Stick to nouns and verbs.

As for doing it Chemda's way, that's your decision. Just don't add the part about getting an STD test if you do in fact have an STD. It's hard to cheat those tests.

Wow! You have to be a retard to not be on the pill? "Mmmm, these are sooo delicious?!" Am *I* dating a child?

Awww . . . baby wants her ba-ba?

Asshole.

My girlfriend won't go down on me. Can I convince her to change her mind?

People who don't like oral sex usually can't be convinced otherwise. They have an aversion to the act. Personally, I would dump someone who thought any of the basic sexual acts were "icky." But I have my priorities and you have yours. How much does it matter to you that your penis will never go in someone's mouth again?

We're accepting she won't suck your dick? Do they even make women like that anymore?

Pretend your dick is an airplane and her mouth is a hangar. "We're comin' in low tonight."

Actually, I've been with more than a few women who needed to be told I liked my dick sucked. It's shocking that some women need to be told that all men want blow jobs. Your job now is to bring it up in bed. As you're fucking and talking dirty, it's not out of line to say, "God I need my cock in your mouth." I bet she makes a beeline straight to D-town.

After she's done, put sticker stars on her forehead rating her one to five stars. (*Everyone* likes sticker stars.)

If there's no way of changing her mind, leave her. Don't bother telling her why, because that will seem petty. Even if she decided to suck your dick now to keep you two together, the blow jobs are going to be the saddest, most pathetic knob jobs ever performed. Just cut and run now.

I have no idea how to touch my girlfriend enough to please her. Am I missing something?

While it can seem very difficult to figure out a woman's body sometimes, it is not impossible. Women (and humans in general) communicate a good amount through body language. You know when to kiss someone by the way she looks at you, and you will lean in without consciously thinking about it. By looking for body language clues, you will know where and with what pressure to touch her. More than likely she has been physically hinting at you for a while now. Aside from trying to read her body, you can also ask her how she likes what you're doing. It's okay to talk about what you're doing as you're doing it. It, actually, can get pretty hot and add to the whole experience.

No, you're not missing something. What might be throwing you off is that in your last relationship your girlfriend thought your touch was like the Lord's Himself. Now you're with this new girl, and every move is wrong. You touch her one way, and it hurts. Another, and it tickles. The problem is that every girl is different. You have to unlearn and relearn everything. It's a little game these bitches decided on back in the Caveman Days. Everyone's different so they can feel special. Back to the drawing board.

I broke up with my boyfriend about a year ago and ran into him the other day. I still have his contact info. Is it wrong to sleep with him one more time?

If you're both on the same page, why not? If you didn't break up over domestic abuse, I say go for it. People are always hanging out with people despite thinking they are half assholes just to have someone to hang out with. Why can't you fuck a guy you already fucked before to get laid?

Just be sure that this time you're willing to suck his dick.

I assume that the reason that you broke up is not because of the sex, since you want to give that a go again. Here's the test: Think about all the things that you were angry about when you broke up a year ago. Think about how long it took you to be okay with hearing his name mentioned. Think about all of that occurring again, since history so often repeats itself. Now ask yourself this: Can you really not get anyone else to fuck you?

Stop moving backward. Put on your pretty clothes and some lip gloss, and go out and find someone you can make new drama with.

My partner is like a dead fish when we have sex. How can I make her more involved?

Telling someone that you want a change or an add-on in the sex department usually makes people nervous. The fear is that you might offend your partner and make them think that they are not satisfying you and haven't been for the entire relationship. If this is how you feel, and that's the reason you can't just outright tell your girlfriend that you would like for her to be more involved, then try this: The next time you have sex with her, whisper in her ear how good it feels to be inside her and how great it is to hold her body. Ask her if she feels the same way. Then talk about how you love her hips. How fantastically sexy they look and feel. Then put your hands on her hips and hold on. Move them to the flow that yours are moving to and tell her how great it feels when she moves like that. In doing that, you will teach her what kind of movements you crave and how to do them. Try to get her to speak back to you so that she gets more comfortable expressing herself during sex. Use the same technique in other positions.

I gotta go jerk off . . .

My wife comes to bed in her oldest, most torn-up clothing. I know that she's comfortable, but I would love for her to care about her appearance in bed. Am I being inconsiderate?

It's very easy to get lazy in many areas of the relationship after being with each other for a while. Instead of the bedroom being the sex room it once was, your wife (and probably you too) see it more as the place where the bed is. In order for your wife to care about what she wears in the bedroom, it's possible that a lot of things need to change. For example, if you don't hit on her and get her revved up, then she will not be motivated to get you charged. It's a catch-22. Both of you want to be turned on, and neither one of you is willing to do the necessary work. Since you're the one who wrote in, you take the initiative. Show her that you care about your appearance. Work out; take care of how you look in and out of the house. Even buy some nice pajamas yourself. While your change is happening, compliment her, pay a little more attention to her, and buy her a couple of outfits that you want to see her in when she goes to bed. The extra steps that you take will make her feel sexy. She will want to match your energy and live up to your words and general admiration. She'll be wearing garter belts, teddies, and lace for her pleasure too. Everyone feels like a champion.

All wrong!

Just kidding, it's all right. You get comfortable, and you stop making it clear how into the other person you are. It's nice to think you can take someone for granted, but you still have to show that you care. Give a fuck, and she'll give you fucks.

My boyfriend is eager in bed, but too eager. If I tell him to slow down and work with me, he gets scared and feels inadequate. What the hell? I'm trying hard!

Stop yelling at him! A man's penis is very sensitive. He hears your frustrations even when you're not talking. It's not your fault, though. Somewhere along the line he lost his balance, rhythm, and concentration—everything he needs to work well with you in the sack. Since you've already tried working with him while you're having sex, it's time to do some work outside the bedroom. He has to own up to needing some help, and you have to help him find what he needs to get better. Together, you can look up some information online, watch some porn together for inspiration, even go to see a sex therapist for some advice. Sex is a very important thing in a relationship. It affects how people respond to one another both emotionally and physically.

While his eagerness is a weird compliment to you, he does need to curb his behavior. Understand that hearing he's bad at sex is probably the most devastating thing in his life, even over a parent's death or a job loss. That is not a joke or an exaggeration. Be sure to tell him what he's doing correctly, praise him when he does well, and, like Chemda said, be sure that he understands that you're both in the fight together.

My boyfriend and I have been dating for three years. He just brought up the idea of a threesome. I used to mess around with my girlfriend, so I thought that maybe she could be the third. Is this a mistake?

The only hang-up would be that if something went bad in your head after the threesome (for example, you feel your man was more into her than you), you might not enjoy the company of your girl-friend anymore. But only you know if you and her (and your man) can handle that.

I don't believe wanting a three-way means you're missing something in your heart. I enjoy steak, chicken, and pizza, but every now and again a nice bagel and lox is a fantastically delicious change of pace. The next day, I'm still anxious to eat the hamburger.

The point is: Who's to say what's wrong? If you're mature enough to do it, you're mature enough to do it. If anyone feels weird, even for a minute, stop. If you have a great time, e-mail me the pictures.

Keith is right. No one can decide this for you. Think of the consequences in your head and decide what you think might happen if, for example, he moans differently with your friend than he does with you. Make sure that you're not doing this just to please him, but rather because you are excited by this as well. Keep in mind that it doesn't *have* to be your friend. It might be better to have someone involved that you never have to see again. This way you don't have to worry about who's thinking what when you're all in the room again days after the three-way. You have a lot of options. Try to think of all the angles before jumping in.

Fine, I'll do it.

My girlfriend's mother hit on me. She's really hot and said that she would keep the affair between us. Should I go for it?

Should you go for it? Sure. Why not? Of course she won't tell. She's obviously a very trustworthy person.

Mommy sounds a little nutty. Can you imagine your dad sleeping with your girlfriend? Oh, you can? Then seriously, you and this girl's mom make a great pair.

This is one of those questions that you know the answer to but you want someone to back you up so that you don't feel as guilty. Obviously, if you respect your girlfriend and want to keep her you will stay away from her mom.

If you're even considering banging your girl's mom then not only do you want to do it but you will not stop thinking about it until you do. It's either do the mom or wait until your girlfriend gets to be her age and hope that she looks like her. Do your girl a favor and do her mom. Then you can focus on the beautiful relationship you have with the daughter, you idiot.

I don't know how to talk dirty. Is it possible to learn this?

You need on-the-job training.

I love it. I love to talk dirt and hear dirt. It's filthy, and it's fun. But I wasn't born doing it. You would think I was by the word on the street, but I really wasn't. I had to awkwardly throw a phrase or two out there to get the confidence I have today. Start simple, see that the other person's into it also, push the envelope, and you're home free.

"You like getting fucked?" That's a safe and simple one. Chances are they do like getting fucked since they're already fucking. After they respond in the affirmative, throw out another one. "You like my cock/pussy?" Again, chances are they do, but this will bolster your confidence, until soon you're choking the other person as you call them your sweet little bitch. Just remember that your partner is only your slut-cunt in the bedroom, and that outside of the bedroom they deserve respect, as all human beings do. Right? I know I've heard that somewhere.

If even what Keith is suggesting is hard for you to start with because his terms are still more aggressive than you are comfortable with, try something less insistent. First start with sounds. Something like "Mmmm" and "Ohhhh." Listen to the way you sound doing it. Listen to how sexy that sounds, and think about how reassured it's making your partner feel. Once you're comfortable with that, go to simple terms that aren't about him so that you don't have to second-guess his response and worry yourself over it. Say things like "That feels good," and "I like your hand there." There's less fear in those sentences because you're not asking him how he feels, so you're not anxious about a reply. Once you find yourself getting used to saying *anything* in bed, talking during sex becomes easier as you go.

I recently discovered, through watching some new porno, that I'm interested in adding a bit more kink into my sex life. I've been seeing a guy for a few months and the sex is good, but I'm thinking that I want to take it to the next level. How do I tell him that I want to turn up the heat in the bedroom without embarrassing myself?

Without embarrassing yourself? Do you know what you look like as it is? Sex is often silly and weird—the noises, the positions . . . Don't worry, you both already look like a couple of jackasses. Besides, you need to remember that everyone is worrying how *they* come off. They have no idea that you're insecure too.

Go for it.

Sneak the porn that you saw into his collection, and maybe he'll think that he discovered the new moves himself. Then when he comes to you asking if you're into it, act like he's a pervert, but say that you're willing to do it because you love him.

My girlfriend told me she'd like me to pull her hair and generally be more rough when we have sex. I'd like to try to please her, but I have no idea how to be rough with a girl without thinking that I'm hurting her. How can I tell how rough she wants it?

Have a safety word; then you know when things are too much. Barring that, it's a free-for-all. Slap her across the face. See how much this bitch can take. You'd be surprised what girls like and how resilient they can be. You can't have the potential to pop a baby out of your crotch and not be tough.

If you have no clue where to start, then tell your girlfriend that you'd love to get into this new idea, but you want to do it right. Have her show you some porn with the kind of behavior she's looking for. Talk about it while you're watching. Even that can be sexy. If you're watching a girl get deep-throated while being held down, say something like "You like that, dirty girl, don't you? You want me to hold you down like that and hurt you with my cock?" You'll be learning and playing at the same time.

Also, pick up on physical cues. People give them all the time. They mostly don't even know they're doing it. For example, if you're kissing her on her stomach and you feel her pelvic area pushing up, you know she wants your mouth on her pussy. If you touch her hair and she gasps a bit, she wants you to pull hard on it.

Good luck with your adventure, you filthy piece of shit. Oh, you like when I give you nasty advice, don't you? You're so pathetic.

My wife and I used to have sex every day. Now it seems like she's doing me a favor when she decides to *let me* do anything physical with her once a week if I'm lucky. I heard of sex diminishing after marriage, but this is ridiculous. Is this the life that I'll be leading or is there something I can do about it?

She's comfortable with you, your sex has become ho-hum, and because it's no big deal if she fucks you or not, she figures, "Why bother? I'm only gonna need a shower."

Millions upon millions of people watch sitcoms that focus around a husband-and-wife team—some good (*Everybody Loves Raymond*) and some awful (every single other one). These shows are being watched because people can relate. Well, here's what you need to do to keep your life from becoming *The King of Queens:* Do something Doug Heffernan wouldn't do. Do something anyone on ABC wouldn't do. Start being the TV show you'd rather live. They're fucking over there on Showtime a lot. You know why? Cause they don't sulk and then have boring sex. They get home and ravage and have fun—fucking that's worth taking the time from folding laundry. And people are relating to these shows, too. In fact, often, paid cable programs have bigger audiences than the biggest shows the networks have to offer. So, I ask you: Which show are you?

Give it to your wife like she's the mistress. You'll get that old whore back in no time.

Well, look out ladies! Looks like I'mma have me a good life.

I recently started a company. I work from home. My wife commutes to her job. I've been stressing so much about my new business that I lost my sex drive. I used to be excited to see my wife when we got home from work. I hate to admit it, but now I just think she's an interruption to my day. I don't know how to find the balance between my wife and my new career. Am I going to lose my marriage over this?

Starting a new company weighs heavily on a person. That's completely normal. In order to find a balance, you have to create one. You have to set hours for home and work even when work is in your home. Try to set your hours around your wife's schedule as much as possible. Start working when she leaves the house and finish about a half hour before she gets home. That half hour will give you time to switch gears from entrepreneur to husband. If you need more work time, after spending some time with your wife, you can get back to your business. Being with your wife is not only important for the obvious reasons, but it also helps you keep from getting burned out from all the stress of building a company. This way you get to keep your new venture and your wife instead of watching both slip away.

It's not like *POOF!* you don't like sex anymore. You just forgot about it. Take a second and throw on a porn, drip a little lotion . . . Oh, looks like someone's back. Good for you, Showtime!

My girlfriend mentioned that she wants to role-play in the bedroom. I'm very willing to try, but I don't want to look stupid. I can't imagine putting on some cowboy gear and an accent and having her not laugh at me. Is there a way to do this without looking or sounding stupid?

Role-playing has the potential to make anyone look silly. (Am I helping yet?) Role-playing does not have to be full gear, fake mustache and lasso. It can start with whispering ideas of a role in someone's ear. For example, if you were watching a movie with your girlfriend and she liked one of the male characters, you can bring that up during sex later. Talk to her as if she was the love interest of the character she liked. This way, she gets to play a role just as easily as you do, and you don't have to feel like you're out there all by yourself.

Be sure to play the exciting part of the movie, when everything's working out between the couple and they're banging on the roof. This isn't the time to test out your high school acting lessons by remaking the scene where the guy couldn't afford to feed the family.

I saw my girlfriend's favorite vibrator, and I am in shock. It's huge! It's got things that swirl and two things that vibrate. How the hell can a man please this person, ever?!

I use a vibrator when Keith is not available. I would replace a vibrator with a human any day. The reason I use a device when masturbating is not because I don't think a real man can please me, it's because it helps me please myself when I'm by myself.

You just have to believe me when I say you can. I understand why it looks overwhelming. I felt the same way as you. But there's something about a live cock that still thrills them the most. My dick doesn't have bulging black plastic veins or beads that circle its head, but it does have blood that pumps from my heart, and something about that keeps them going.

I guess look at it this way: I've used fake vaginas and fake mouths—synthetic stuff that's supposed to feel real. You can fuck that and not be criticized for making any wrong move, you can come wherever you want, and when you're done no one's asking you any follow-up questions. Yet, despite all the positives, a real pussy is better. Why? Something about it being alive.

My girlfriend saw an ad for a local amateur strip contest. The winner gets one thousand dollars. She's really excited to do it, and I think she can win. She's smokin' hot, and she's a dancer. Thing is, I don't know if I feel comfortable with other guys looking at my girlfriend in that way. I feel like I want her to keep that kind of stuff between us. Should I let her do it?

If you don't think that you will be comfortable with her stripping, then you won't be. It might help to not go with her the night of the contest. It's likely, though, that even thinking about the potential of what is happening while she's dancing will drive you nuts. You have to decide if this is worth putting your foot down for, and she has to decide how much this contest means to her.

You're not a fun guy. It's not your fault. You were born that way.

Tell her you can't handle it, because you can't. The end.

Money

Keith and I have had issues with money throughout our dating experience. Though we don't see ourselves as very money-oriented, money has affected our relationship so much that it influenced the first time we said "I love you" to each other. Money problems weighed so hard on us that at one point they nearly caused a breakup.

When Keith and I first met, he had no job, no money, and no apparent desire to get either. I was working three jobs at the time and still struggling to pay for the house that I'd just bought. Our differing employment prospects didn't bother me, though, because I was not thinking of Keith as a long-term relationship. I figured we would have some fun and then move on. Keith was easy to hang out with—incredibly funny and fantastic to be around. We had fun as I anticipated, but we did not move on. About three months into the relationship, we had declared our connection official and were very excited to be together. However, I was still skeptical. I was concerned about his intentions. He still didn't have a job, he was broke, he started owing money, and he was about to have no place to live. I was able to hook him up with one of my part-time jobs doing some entertaining as a clown for children's parties. I kept him in mind when shopping for groceries, and I offered him a temporary stay at my place until he found a permanent home. During his stay, we got closer. That's when, after frequently staring into each other's eyes and making like we were about to say something, he said it.

"I love you."

"Well," I replied, "I would love me, too, but you can't say that until you don't *need* me to exist."

And that was our first expression of adoration. Ain't love grand?

Obviously, this is not the romantic story every girl dreams of, but, eventually, the bastard got a job and started paying his share, and we planned on permanently living together. Unfortunately, that did not last long. His job did not always pay enough, and he kept getting more and more behind on bills that he now shared with me. We talked about it several times—and by *talked* I mean I made it clear that this was not okay by me and that he really needed to get his act together. He would hang his head in shame and tell me he would do better. Though I knew he had good intentions, his intentions were not paying any portion of what he owed. I finally had to put my foot down and set a date. If he did not get a job and find a way to catch up by that date, he would have to move out and we would have to talk about whether our relationship could sustain the blow. The reasoning behind my anger was more than money owed on bills—it was that he was not doing everything he could and I was struggling to pay for bare necessities. It was not the bills that were bothering me as much as his lack of motivation to help me. That was not and is not what I consider love.

Luckily, things got better, and Keith made more efforts. We still have a hard time with money, but at this point we're equally to blame. We're not the best budget setters, as we have a great time justifying a two-hundred-dollar dinner together.

People talk about how money is not important, but rather it

is really health and happiness that you should strive for. However, money is one of the most common reasons why marriages end. So, when lovers get together, they need to talk about this taboo topic. How people make and spend their money is very telling. That is not to say that a person's job defines them, but it may reveal some personality traits such as a person's drive, interests, and opportunities. Not knowing your partner's relationship with money is not knowing them completely.

I hate how I learned this lesson, but I love that he finally did too.

My bad.

Get back to work!

MONEY Questions

Whose responsibility is it to pay on the first date?

It used to be a given that the man would always pay. First date, second, always. The reason this standard was set was because women either were not working at all or were working and getting paid one-fourth of a man's salary. Now that women are regulars in the workplace with wages comparable to men's, there are new dating customs. A popular trend seems to be that the person who initiates the date pays for it. However, though standards have changed, the male ego has not evolved at the same rate, and paying for a date still seems to set a man in a more comfortable zone. Whether you care about that or not is your choice.

Rich or not, these women want you to pay for that date. A free meal never went out of style.

I've been with my girlfriend for two years now. We recently got engaged, which, understandably, started a lot of very intense conversations about our future, one of which is whether we should have a joint bank account or not. I'm a bit hesitant about it, but I'm wondering if I'm wrong and this decision is inevitable and part of the marriage process. What do you think about joint bank accounts?

I get the idea of both—a joint bank account for joint things, a separate bank account for separate things. So there you have it. Have both. Keep your independence. You can feel like a man with your own money at a strip club, and now how much money you spent won't be an argument the next day. You'll only have to answer for why your balls smell like whore.

Chemda and I share everything, but I like opening my own mail, for example. I'm completely with her, but yet I still like the idea that I have some things that are for me. Of course this mail is usually bills that I then want her to pay half of, but I think you see my point.

Get both. Have your freedom, and understand you now share your life with another. Plus, separate bank accounts make giving gifts actually surprising and nice.

In getting married you are saying that everything is shared: emotions, time, bank accounts, etc. . . . That being said, I too believe in some separation, and that includes money. Have a joint bank account, and have a personal one. That joint bank account can contain money for your bills and the money that you allot for shared spending. Every month, both of you can put your share into the joint bank account and leave what's left in your own, obviously reassessing here and again what that number is. This solution not only saves on fights, since the required spending is taken care of, but now no one can get upset when one spends money on something like expensive shoes. It also lends itself to romance, since money for something like flowers is not bought out of shared cash.

By the way, I see that my examples are very sided toward benefiting the woman. That was not a coincidence. Feel free to use my shoe/flowers explanation in your approach. You of course are free to use Keith's stripper example instead. You know your wife best.

My husband makes financial sacrifices that make no sense. We are a middle-class family living well and making a decent amount of money. We both have great jobs and are financially comfortable. For some reason, despite these facts, my husband feels the need to hoard money as if we may never see another dime in our lives. He refuses to ever eat out. He won't go to the movies because renting DVDs is cheaper. He even eats things after their expiration date because he thinks throwing them out is the same as throwing out money. His attitude not only grates

on my nerves, but it also affects my happiness. How do I get him to worry less about money and take me out once in a while?

Rob him! He clearly can afford it.

Your husband will never be as comfortable with spending money as you are. It's a personality trait that is ingrained. The solution to this is to set a budget that you both can agree on. Set a monthly allowance that the two of you can spend on frivolous and fun experiences. To him, every purchase you make seems like it's a never-ending pit of spending. Seeing an allotted amount sets a limit that should make money matters a little easier for him to handle.

It's fairly simple. His worry about the economy fluctuating so wildly ensures that—

Oh, quiet. Like you know anything about money.

My husband thinks I spend too much money on frivolous things. I make just as much as he does. Can he really tell me what to do with my paycheck?

If he decides that strip clubs and paintball trips are not frivolous, will you have the same attitude? Huh? Will you? If you get to not have an opinion on any of his purchases ever, then yes, you're right.

Yes, he can. You actually signed a contract about intertwining your life. Remember that day? What you can agree on is an allowance for the both of you where you each get the same amount for personal things, be they "frivolous" or not.

I just started dating a girl whom I really like, but I can't afford to keep taking her out. What do I do?

Not every romantic thing is expensive. Be a little more creative. Cooking dinner is cheaper than going out, and most girls will appreciate the effort. Can't cook? Have her teach you, or learn together. Things like a "spontaneous" walk in the park, a bubble bath, or a handmade card are some of the most impressive moves to make.

You set too high a precedent. REDO! Dump her, and start over with someone else. And this time act like you know how to read a bank statement. This relationship wasn't going anywhere anyway. Don't kid yourself.

If I know that he's going to want to pay for dinner anyway, do I still reach for the check and pretend to want to pay?

This is a weird one. I know I'm paying, you know I'm paying, and the waiter knows I'm paying. The whole town knows I'm paying. But if you just sit there when the check comes on any early dates, guys will think you expect us to cover everything and that we're being taken advantage of. However, if you take out your purse, of course we'll convince you not to chip in. Thing is, we mean it. We *do* want to pay. It's in our DNA. We just need you to recognize that we're paying, and that you don't really think something magical happened to the check. So yes, pretend to go for the money (but really *have* money, don't mime it), and we'll all play our dumb game.

Then again, maybe you're out with the cheap-ass from the last question. This is a good way to find out. Go for your money, and if he doesn't stop *you*, just pay the bill and "go to the bathroom." This relationship wasn't going anywhere anyway. Don't kid yourself.

It depends on how great of an actress you are. No one likes a bad liar.

I gambled way more than my wife and I agreed to on a recent trip to the casino. What can I do to get me out of the trouble facing me at home due to this mistake?

First off, don't buy her flowers on the way home. That's just spending more money that you can't afford thanks to your bender.

You can't win this one. You fucked up. The best thing to do would be to go home and tell the truth and take the pain coming to you. If you act at all defensive about it, you can forget her ever forgiving you. If you really want to make things better, get a temporary side job to help get your finances in a better state.

How interesting. I bet if you risked more but *won* it'd be okay.

First of all, don't show weakness. You messed up, but you didn't kill somebody. Deal with it the way you'd deal with a hurt child. For the most part, kids don't cry after a bad fall unless you baby them. Same thing with adults. "Well eff me, the casino got me. I feel dumb. I know I'll never do that again. I'm an a-hole." Punish yourself before she punishes you. "No guys' nights out this month for me. Damn. Lesson learned. I need to listen to you more . . . Can I make dinner?"

My wife makes more money than me. She never throws it in my face, but I can't help but feel like less of a man. Is this normal?

Yes, it's normal to feel weird, but try to keep in mind that your wife is not getting paid more than you just to hurt your precious feelings. And when she gets you that set of golf clubs you "always wanted," just know that she saved you a few extra shifts of overtime.

Yes, it's normal. It's normal because you're supposed to feel that way. Since Adam was a caveman, guys were the supporters. It's a new world, and women can work too, but it's not natural for the woman to be making more than the man. Get a better job. I had to get a job to keep my woman, and you need a better one to respect yourself. In fact, my girl thinks we're fifty-fifty in everything we do because we work together. Little does she know I own 51 percent of this book, and she 49. Yes, I will take out the garbage and build another shelf, but only because I know I'm a real man.

My wife and I are very social and love spending time with our friends. A big part of that time is spent entertaining guests in our home. We go out of our way to please our company and that includes buying food, drink, and entertainment. The problem is that I'm afraid that not all the visits fit into our budget. My wife insists that the only way to throw any party is to make it elaborate, but I think some finger food and a couple of drinks will do. Every time I bring this up, we get into a fight and nothing gets resolved. I don't want to have our parties put us into the poorhouse. How can I make my wife understand that small-scale ideas can still be fun?

Your wife is the one who puts these parties together, and she's very afraid of disappointing. Chemda's the same. She could slave over homemade steak and shrimp fajitas with all the fixings, but if the guacamole (which she doesn't even enjoy) comes out "too chunky," or—God forbid—she realizes that she forgot to make black beans, everything is a failure. "Oh my God, I put salmon, corn, and yellow rice on the same plate! The food was all the same color!" Like anyone noticed or gave a shit. She's the same way when it comes to spending money on parties, which is why I decided to throw my own parties, where she can't get involved. At first it gave her cold sweats to see my buddies only eating regular sandwiches and beer, but soon she realized that everyone was enjoying themselves just the same, and I never looked like an asshole. Now you don't get Dom Pérignon, you get generic white wine. Everyone still has a great time. We haven't lost a guest yet.

 Time to turn into an accountant. It's easy to get carried away with spending when you don't know how much of it you're doing and how much of it is affecting you. What you need to do is look at last month's spending. Make a note of how much of that was spent on entertaining. Make a couple more notes on how much you both brought in and what bills and other mandatory spending you share. Bring these numbers to your wife. Make sure that you are not coming from an angry place. The goal is to look at the numbers and decide what would actually be feasible for spending on parties. With actual figures in hand, it will not be an emotional argument; it will include more logic and fact.

My husband and I have been married for five years. Things have been great. Our lives are simple. We both work. He's an accountant, and I'm a schoolteacher. We are now both in our early thirties, which is when we planned on starting a family. However, instead of talking about having babies, my husband decided that now is a good time to start a band. He claims that he finally has the time and money to invest in something he's always wanted, and that I am selfish if I can't see that this is his dream. This band idea is new to me and is really distracting from what we originally planned on. I feel like he will be wasting money and time that would otherwise go toward our future with our children. Can I deter what seems like my husband's early midlife crisis?

Your husband sounds like an idiot, but he's also trying to tell you something. He doesn't want a baby. Not now, possibly not ever, possibly just not with you. Though it's a shitty way of expressing anything—and he is letting you down by not following the plans that you both set out for—things are what they are. If you keep your head buried and you don't see the shift, you will only be setting yourself up for the inevitable, which will be even more painful and drawn out. Get to the heart of the problem and it will be easier in the long run.

Have him send me a demo. I'll get to the bottom of this.

My wife loves it when I buy her gifts. Not just on her birthday and holidays, but she likes the surprise of me coming home with a present. I understand that this is standard practice and I'd like to accommodate her, but does she not see when our account is depleted? We have a joint bank account. We both have access to it. Why does my wife need presents when we're having trouble paying bills?

The next gift you give her should be a Tiffany box with past-due bills inside.

Your wife needs to grow up. She clearly wants your affection and proof that you think about her. She needs to learn a different way to get this reassurance. Because you're the one who sees the situation more clearly, you have to be the teacher here. Tell her about your stress regarding your bank account and paying bills. Make sure that she knows that you love her and that flowers are not proof. At the same time, be ready with a couple of examples to share with her of other things that you are willing to do that are not financially burdening—such as writing her a sweet letter, planning a picnic, preparing dinner—anything that you are capable and comfortable with that shows that you thought about her and put effort into expressing it. And she can do the same in return. Last I checked, blow jobs are still free.

When my husband and I first got married, we naturally assigned ourselves certain household duties. One of mine is taking care of the bank-related responsibilities. I deposit checks, withdraw what we need and pay bills, et cetera. Every once in a while, we get a bit low in our account. At this point, I tell my husband to not use his bank card for anything, as it could overdraw the account easily. He's normally a very intelligent man, so why does my husband not understand how a bank works?

There's a reason you took on this role. It's because he really doesn't get it. This will not end. Keith has done this several times. It's as if he thinks the bank account will understand that he wasn't thinking at that moment. What I want to do is take his bank card when we have this issue, but iTunes already has his info, and spending money is just a click away. And that's another thing! He'll blame iTunes for being so convenient! I say every time they fuck up like this they owe us a massage.

Overdrawing the account? I think *somebody* snuck in their own question . . . Oh, Chemda . . .

It's Missile Command! Old school and new! In one program! That you can play on your phone! And I can win it by pressing one button!

I don't know why I forget. I'll try to be better. It's just your department, and that's why I get absentminded about it.

I'll make it up to you. Last I heard, eating pussy is still free.

I said *massage*. You still don't listen . . .

My wife recently decided that she "needs" our kitchen to be fully redone. To me, the kitchen seems perfectly functional and aesthetically pleasing. She claims it's not modern and can use some updates. To be honest, she uses the kitchen way more than I do. I feel odd saying no to her because she's the one who cooks and takes care of that room in the house. However, we don't have the money to make this change. Why would my wife want a better kitchen in exchange for huge financial burdens?

Your wife is being frivolous and ridiculous. You spend more time on the toilet; should you be asking for a redo on that? Tell your wife that if she shows you how to pay for the kitchen without getting a loan or dipping into funds that are obviously meant for existing bills, you can start talking about it.

Personally, I say you let her do it. Fuck it; get into debt. But then go with what Chemda was alluding to: Fix up your bathroom. Get a nice leather chair that functions as a toilet. I saw a toilet paper roll holder/iPhone dock. Picture that! You're playing poker on your iPhone, you have pocket deuces, and you're dropping a deuce! Then turn on the bidet, and get a nice splash up the keister while you beat Missile Command.

Then again, I don't know anything about money. Chemda could be right.

My husband and I always planned on having our firstborn just before we reach the age of thirty. We are now inching toward that time, but I feel like we're not ready yet. We both still have student loans to finish paying, and we're still working to have better and more stable positions in our respective careers. I know we set these goals and that it's important to follow through on promises and meet targets that we set for ourselves, but shouldn't we wait to afford kids before we have them?

If you're not ready to have a baby, then you're not ready. However, since this is a big goal for you, make it happen. Don't just wait for you and your husband to have the money. Plan on what will make that happen. For the next year or so, respond financially as if you have a baby. For example, set aside the money that you would have to pay for diapers, food, and day care if you'll need it. This will grow your savings account or let you know that you're either not ready or need another job. Make the commitment for the goal that you've set for yourself, or it will never happen.

Skip it. Babies are assholes. You want to know something? True story: I don't have one friend who's a baby. I have friends of all races and creeds; no friends who are babies. Something to think about.

My wife drives me nuts sometimes with her frugal ways. One of my big pet peeves is that she keeps buying only the generic brand in the store. I feel like the products are inferior and that we end up saving a bit on money but losing a lot in quality. Is there any way to change a cheap mind?

You can't change that she's cheap, but you can open your mind up to a couple of things and compromise. Some generic items are really cheap in quality and make no sense to buy, because they fall apart and need to be replaced too often. However, some generic products are exactly the same as the name brands without the fancy packaging. Look at labels and ingredients for the products that your wife buys. Find out which ones are the same products as the pretty-packaged ones. Once you have your list of things you are willing to compromise on, it will be easier to ask her to meet you halfway.

Fair is fair. She can get some things generic, but yes: No to generic peanut butter, toilet paper, garbage bags, and powdered milk. Tell her, "You want to start your day with a nice bowl of Fruit Circles or Sugared Flakes, that's okay; however, I am still a human, and I took the time to make a list regarding the standard of living I've been accustomed to."

I'm in love with my boyfriend. He's great. We love each other a lot, and we recently started talking about our relationship's potential for marriage. My big concern about this is that I know his credit is downright awful. I worked very hard to keep my record perfect, and I feel like attaching myself to him will take my credit down. How important is it to consider your partner's credit potential when considering marriage?

Not important at all?

It is important, but not deal breaking. Credit can be fixed. He needs to get a good financial advisor and devise a plan with them that will be most efficient in fixing his financial situation. From there it's just about how much your partner wants to commit to the change. Feel free to judge him based on that.

My wife recently got a receptionist job in an office in the fashion industry. She has since started buying fancy and expensive-labeled clothing that we cannot afford on our salaries. She claims that the office requires her to keep up with fashion, but I claim that they then need to pay her accordingly. How do I keep from going to the poorhouse over some guy's name on my wife's blouse's tag?

Your wife took a job that doesn't pay. If you are required by the company that you work for to dress beyond your means, then your paycheck is a joke. As I'm sure you suspect, your wife might be using her job as an excuse to spend too much money on clothing. You have to show your wife that things are not adding up financially, and her new position does not make up for new clothing. Take her pay stubs and the receipts for the new clothing, crunch the numbers, and bring the results to her. If that doesn't work, then take her credit cards before she runs you into the ground. Give them back after she learns math.

According to every single daytime talk show, there are a lot of designer knockoffs that completely fool people, and, "You too can look like Sarah Jessica Parker for as little as fifteen dollars!" If at her job they realize she's substituting crap for name-brand styles and they fire her, have her write a letter to the *Today* show explaining how they're all fuckin' liars and demand that Matt Lauer give her a job.

My husband feels the need to have bottled water delivered to us. We live in an area where tap water is considered some of the best in the country, but he insists on spending money on these bottles. He says that he likes the taste of the water better, and that the bottles are convenient for him. Though we can afford it, I hate to see money wasted like that. Is there any way to win this battle?

It's hard to see money wasted, but in this case, you might have to cut your husband a break. If the bottled water is making him happy, then compromise. The ease that this will bring you is better than saving a couple of dollars. Plus, there have got to be a few things that he's seeing you do that he knows you can do without. For example: manicures and pedicures, eyebrow shapings, massages, et cetera. Whatever your splurge is that he can't participate in is not going unnoticed.

I can't convince you that there's a taste difference between bottled water and good tap water, but I'm a firm believer that there is, and I'm a bottled water buyer. In fact, I can sometimes tell the difference between one brand of bottled water and another.

Regardless of whether you think I'm right or a jackass, you need to follow Chemda's advice. This is his silly pleasure, and the stuff like massages that she mentioned is your thing. Enjoy your shit water, don't be surprised when your babies are born out of your asshole, and let him do his thing.

My husband is talking about quitting his job. He's miserable at work every day. His boss is mean, and his coworkers are back-stabbing. I feel for him, but I also know that we cannot afford for him to be out of work. I don't want him to be unhappy. What is the right decision here?

Your husband can't just quit his job. That's not how life works. I know that you feel for him, and you want to alleviate his misery, but this is not the way to do it. If he quits his job and doesn't get another one right away, then his misery will become worse, as will yours. It's a difficult time for him, so instead of giving him a quick solution that doesn't fix anything, help him find a better job. You and he can get together after work every day and go through all the resources there are for job hunting. Your encouragement with pushing forward will mean more in the long run to the both of you.

The problem with people is that they don't look for something better unless they're desperate. I've been guilty of it too. We all have. Sure, your husband isn't happy, but he's still getting a steady paycheck, and that's keeping him from sending out résumés; however, now is really the time to strike. Because he has money coming in, he won't seem so desperate in job interviews. Employers can tell when you absolutely *need* them, and they'll either not hire you or take advantage of you.

"I need you to clean out the gutters, and we'll pay you ten dollars a day and all the chitlins you can eat."

"I'll take it!"

He needs to look for something new, now, before he has nothing and settles for something even worse. He needs to think things through. He's not a baby.

My husband deserves a raise at work, but he's too shy to ask for it. How do I get him to toughen up and ask for what's rightfully his?

 It's nice to think you'll get what you deserve in this world, but either the company's trying to save money or his raise got lost in the shuffle. (I'm sure they're not passing over him because he does shoddy work. Perish the thought.)

I was in the military, and one time I didn't get a promotion to a higher rank when it was due simply because I was forgotten. It wasn't out of spite or because of my lack of skill. I knew I was a great soldier. And even if I wasn't exceptional, the rules were simple: I was in for so long, so I should have gotten the next grade. Eventually I said something, and I got my higher rank and pay, including back pay and an apology.

Your man needs to grow a pair. Maybe the company simply forgot. He's afraid to make waves, but if he's earned his raise, there's no shame in going to collect it. Then, again, if you think he's lying about how well he's been doing and that he should just keep quiet and thank his lucky stars he even has a desk, you might not want to push him so hard.

 If your husband deserves a raise, then you're right; he should ask for one. His shyness is preventing him from furthering his life and yours. Most likely, it's the confrontation aspect of the request that he's having trouble with, and that might be too hard for him to let go of. Tell your husband that he can write out all the reasons why he thinks he needs a raise, and then he can ask his boss for a meeting. When he goes into the meeting he can say something like "I would like to submit a request, and I would appreciate it if you looked at what I have outlined." It's not the boldest approach, but the task will get done.

My ten-year wedding anniversary is coming up, and I want to get my wife a more elaborate gift this year. Unfortunately I can't afford it, but I am willing to take a temporary second job for it. Is this a good idea?

The only hang-up is that your woman might start wondering where you're really spending all your time, and she may think you're having an affair. She'll feel weird and uneasy as she thinks about this day after day. About the time she finally confronts you as a lying adulterer, you whip out the gift, and you say, "Happy anniversary. I was working my ass off at a second job for this." She'll start crying, but you continue. "I thought it'd be a nice surprise, but fuck me, I guess . . . somehow I'm a piece of shit."

When she goes for the gift, you quickly snatch your hand away. "I don't think so," you say. Then turn and leave out the door. Go to the local watering hole and share your story with any female who will listen. You won't even have to give up the gift to get some play. If your bitch wife thinks you're a cheater, then fine, you'll show her what cheating's all about!

Go back home at the end of the night and give your wife the gift after all. You might as well. You busted your hump for it. Collect a blow job from her, quit your new job, and enjoy a wife who thinks she owes you not only because of your gift, but also because of remorse and guilt.

If you pull this off she will be very happy, until she realizes how much you were able to consistently sneak off without her knowing. She will be made well aware of what a great liar you are. She'll still appreciate the gift, and her friends will talk about how great it was that you took on this endeavor just for her, but expect to be watched a little more carefully from now on.

Household

Girls were girls and men were men. Those *were* the days . . .

Not anymore. Now girls wear ties, men wear dresses, and this whole world is upside down. It's not bad, it's just different. Women work alongside men, black people are president, and any yahoo can run a radio station out of their house. Things have changed. You used to get married, the man went to work, and the woman cleaned the house and raised the kids. The man came home to a scotch and a foot massage, and everyone was content. Nope, not anymore . . . Now both parents are hitting the pavement, men are becoming Mr. Moms, and everyone is pitching in wherever they can.

It's not bad. It's just different.

It was always important to get to know how to coexist with your mate, but now there is even more to learn, because there are no longer standard roles for genders to play in the household. Does one person like company and the other doesn't? Does one person think it's socially acceptable to visit the other in the bathroom and the other doesn't? Does Chemda sleep like the number four in bed and take up all the room, leaving Keith no room as he shivers and shakes without any covers?

Some things we do in our relationships are by choice, but other things we need to realize we do because of how we were born. I, for example, will never be the chef of the house. This isn't by choice. I was born this way.

Making a sandwich is cooking to me. The meat, the cheese . . . now *lettuce*? You have to open the bread bag, take out the bread, close the bread bag . . . Don't even get me started on if you want the sandwich to be hot. Forget the whole thing. I'm tired already.

Chemda used to try to show me how easy it is to cook. She'd tell me how she made a chicken quesadilla, as if anything she could ever say about food prep would ever register with me.

"And it doesn't get any easier! So easy to make!"

"Good to know. I'll be in the living room."

"But, Keith, it's so easy!"

"Good then. I'll be watching TV."

Slowly we figured out what we were both good at, what we weren't good at, and how to cohabit with each other. Below we'll answer your questions as we reveal all the ins and outs to staying sane living with a completely other human being. But first, I have to bang some pots and pans together so Chemda "accidentally" gets woken up. I'm getting hungry.

HOUSEHOLD Questions

My girlfriend loves to cook but is so very bad at it. I think it's really sweet that she goes through the work, but the food is inedible. What should I do?

Learn to love salt. Salt drowns out some of that nasty taste that your girlfriend puts in your meals. What does the Heart Association know anyway?

Your girlfriend sounds great, and you are sweet to appreciate her attempts. If you can't bring yourself to tell her your feelings on the matter, then try presents. Since she actually likes to cook, though she stinks at it, you can get her cooking gifts such as the Cooking Channel, cookbooks or, better yet, cooking lessons. If need be, express that these gifts are hobby-related and not improvement issues.

Make her eat it. In fact, take her out to a nice restaurant and show her what food should taste like. If she doesn't see a difference between the restaurant's food and hers, then you're dating someone who is cuckoo anyway. Pick up the waitress and leave your girl with the doggie bag.

My wife is a great woman and is usually very neat. However, she has this bad habit of drinking water from a glass and then putting it in the dish rack when she's done with it as if it's clean. I know that she's not the only person in the world who does this (so maybe it's me that's the weirdo), but I think that's gross. I believe that a cup needs to be washed before getting put anywhere where it is considered to be clean again. Am I right or am I crazy?

The only way I see her point is that she may be thinking it's not gross because you both swap spit as it is; however, I guarantee she sometimes gives these "clean" cups to guests and people other than you. She's lazy, and she's wrong. DEAD WRONG!

Let me talk to her.

Dear Wife,

Your husband is half a hard-on. It's water! Who gives a shit? No one's gonna know except you and Yappy McGee over there. Oh well, whatevs. I guess have a glass on the side that's only for you so that Little Baby's skin doesn't crawl. Jesus Christ . . .

For his birthday you should get him one of those microscopes that let you see all the crawling things on his skin. That's a good week of laughter.

Okay, you can pass the book back now. Thanks.

Sincerely,
Keith

Okay, buddy. I set her straight. You just gotta know how to talk to them; that's all. She should be a little less disgusting. Now go eat that pussy. I'm sure it's spic-and-span.

Despite what Keith thinks, you're not crazy. I think that a cup should be washed after it was put on someone's mouth also. Maybe she thinks her mouth is cleaner than other people's? Some people claim that their dog's mouth is cleaner than any human's. People are dumb.

Tell her that you used to have a friend who went over to someone's house and because your friend drank from the guy's glass, he got herpes. This happened because the guy sipped from your friend's cup. It's a made-up story, but herpes scares everyone and it gets your point across. I'm not a doctor, but I don't see why that couldn't happen, and I bet she won't either.

When my wife and I entertain guests at our house, my wife gets overwhelmed and doesn't enjoy herself. We both spend time preparing for our friends' arrival, but for her, it doesn't end there. She's usually running from the kitchen and back the entire time. It seems like she doesn't get to spend time with our guests. I don't know what she's going nuts about, and she won't let me help her, either. She tells me that she enjoyed herself every time, but I don't see how that can be true. How can I get my wife to relax and enjoy the party?

Chemda does this all the time—in and barely out of the kitchen, doting over guests, making sure everyone's comfortable, et cetera . . . She promises she loves it, and I had to learn to believe her. What a weird thing to lie about, anyway. Make peace with it, and enjoy the appetizers.

Your wife thinks that the only way for people to enjoy themselves is if she runs around like a maniac. As much as you think that that would make her feel like she's being neglected or overworking herself, you're most likely wrong. She likes the idea of taking care of people's needs, and she thinks that the only way to do this is to act like a chicken with its head cut off. What she's not realizing is that she might be making her guests feel uncomfortable. When the host is not at ease, it affects the guests.

Here's a plan: Since you and your wife prepare together before the guests arrive, add another preparation tactic to the list. Have your wife write out what she thinks she will have to run around for later. Check the list and see how much of it can be done ahead of time. Any task left should be reassessed and either deemed necessary or vetoed. Whatever duties are left to be done when the guests are there, divide between the two of you before they arrive. Hopefully, this means that she sits a bit more with the guests, and maybe that will show her how much fun that side of the party is, too.

Is this a hint?

I swear to God, if this fuckin' guy just ruined everything for me . . .

What is wrong with my wife that if there is a small bug in the house, she has to yell for me to come over from the other side of the house to kill it? She is usually a strong, confident woman. Why can't she just throw a shoe at it? By the time I get to the room, the bug or rodent is gone, and then she's freaked out that it's still alive. Why didn't she just kill it herself?

Why do women have PMS? Why do women cry? We can't focus on the questions that can only be answered when we get to the Glory that is Heaven; we can only focus on how we might curb the behavior. Chemda's the same way. Or rather she used to be. She's better now. This will be news to Chemda, but here's what I did: You need to respond to the bugs and mice a little slower each time until your wife realizes that she needs to toughen up or her walls are going to have mice babies. Every time she yelps the bug scream (once you pay attention you'll realize it really is its own sound), you need to save her slower and slower until she starts killing these creatures on her own. When she does, you'll see such a pleased look on her face. They get extremely proud of themselves. You won't get the credit for making her stronger, but you will have fewer roaches in your pasta shelf.

Keith! That better not be what you're doing! I know this is just a silly suggestion for this guy!

Bugs are gross. They look disgusting, they move really fast, and they represent dirty things. As I'm typing this now, I can feel a bug on me just by thinking about how gross these things are. Plus, as vile as bugs are alive, it gets even sicker when you squoosh them: Their insides squirt out, and whatever they call bones crack . . . The best solution to helping your wife with this is to buy her a swatter. The added distance between her and the bug will help her not feel the yuckiness of its body being crushed.

And respond slowly to her screams in the future so that she has time to enjoy her new gift.

Eiw!

My husband doesn't like going out on weekdays because we both have work the next day. However, he always ends up watching TV from the time he comes home until about two A.M. When I ask him about it he says that TV relaxes him, while going out would make him tired for work the following day. How can I get this to change?

It's fair, and he's the norm. When you go out you have to engage. You wouldn't let him just stare at you and your friends as you yapped it up. He probably doesn't even know what he's watching, but he finally has time that's his—not work, not company, not anyone else's. It sounds like it's the weekdays that upset you. It's too bad that there are more weekdays than weekends, but that's the problem with jobs—they really ruin your day.

Just because it's the norm doesn't mean it's right. I get that watching TV is relaxing; however, after getting used to sitting on the couch for too long, your brain gets numb. Too much TV makes you forget how much fun the outside world can be.

If your husband was always like this, then you can't ask him for too much change in this department. That's who you married. If this is a new habit, then he might be in a rut. Pick something that you think he would enjoy, and ask him to do it as a favor to you. Make sure that if you're inviting people, you invite only people he likes and not some of your friends who drive him nuts. If this doesn't work, then it looks like you can't rely on him for weekday outings. Call up your friends and hang out with them.

I keep finding plates and cups in the bathroom after my girl-friend comes for a visit. Is it possible that she's eating in there? Why? How can I bring this up without making it awkward?

I like bringing a drink into the shower. I'm comfortable with it, but I can see why someone would feel a little off about it. Luckily, Keith doesn't care. Maybe it doesn't bother him because I've seen his beer mugs in the bathroom, so I know he likes to partake also. Food, however, is another story. Where would she be eating? There's only one seat in that room.

How can bringing this up not be awkward? It can't. You already feel awkward. You have to bring it up directly and see if you and your lady can make it through an uncomfortable conversation. If you don't bring it up, this topic will still be on your mind, and you'll constantly be thinking ill of her.

What do you mean, Is she eating there? She comes over to see you—at your house—and you don't even know if she's eating in your bathroom or not? Well, how else would dishes with food and lipstick stains end up in there? She's making a plate of food, running your microwave, taking it in the bathroom, and you don't even notice? No matter whose fault it is, end your stupid dopey relationship. Christ . . . You don't even know when she eats in your bathroom.

My wife refuses to open her mail. She gets overwhelmed by sorting, opening, and paying bills. I feel like she's really doing some damage, but she won't budge. How can I get her to change this habit?

I like where her head is at. No news is good news.

Mail is one of those silly things that a lot of people get overwhelmed with. If you're good at opening mail, then congratulations; you are the new Household King of Mail. Take on the responsibility or it won't get done. Even though it's on her to do as well, being stubborn about this is like leaving the dog poo on the carpet because it's not your turn to clean it up.

After you catch up with the mess she made of the postal situation, if you want her to be involved, you have to help her. Start by setting a time that you are comfortable with. Pick every day, every other day, or even once a week to sit and open mail. This way you don't have to feel alone in the process, and she won't get overwhelmed with it since you will be with her.

Keep in mind that if you've been in charge of mail for some time and suddenly, out of the blue, your wife starts running to the mailbox, then she is absolutely, without question, having an affair.

My husband and I have one computer between the two of us. When we come home, we each check our home e-mail and then plan to share it the rest of the night. However, once my husband gets on the computer again, he doesn't get off it. I not

only feel like he is being selfish, but I feel neglected. Am I being too sensitive?

You both need to put a cap on how long you use the computer right before bedtime. No one may use the "one more thing" line after the cap has been reached unless it's a work e-mail of great importance that just came in. Otherwise, he needs to keep in mind that he's an adult, and adults need to learn how to budget their time.

If you're setting time for the computer, then set time for other things as well. Your husband might be on the computer thinking that that's the only thing going for the evening. Though you would like to think that time spent with you is a given, an invitation is usually a good idea. Tell him that you would like to set aside time for something as simple as just being with each other in the living room (or any other room for that matter). Just because he doesn't think about this first doesn't mean it can't be romantic. You can't always wait for your husband to ask you to hang out with him. Sometimes you have to take the initiative.

My husband and I have the same work schedule, and we wake up at the same time, but he seems to need less sleep. He stays up later than me all the time. He still wakes up on time for work, but I am always going to sleep by myself. I know that this affects me, and I think it affects our relationship also. When I ask him to come to bed when I'm heading to sleep, he just says he's not tired. Is there anything I can do about this?

 Stop asking him to come to sleep with you. Instead, invite him to the bedroom for other things (the obvious being sex). Other than sex, you can ask him to just hang out with you for a bit. You can wind down the day together. Set a requested and reasonable time, like a half hour. People respond well to boundaries and he will respect that you are valuing his time.

Keith and I like to play a game called High/Low before we go to sleep. The details of this are included in the final chapter of this book.

 Start a blow job when he's on the couch. Finish it in bed.

My girlfriend likes to walk in on me in the bathroom. I tried locking the door, but she will talk to me through the door and get offended that I am not wanting to discuss whatever is on her mind at the moment. Is this worth breaking up over?

 No, you just have to teach her that her behavior is wrong. This is surprisingly simple to do. As much as she thinks that couples should share everything— even the smell of your waste—she still likes being seen as a lady to you. When she's in the bathroom doing *her* duty (LOL), barge in and start talking to her. Quickly overexaggerate how disgusting the stench is.

"Did we eat all the lasagna when— Holy cow, baby! Wow! I guess *you* ate all the lasagna! Holy shit!"

She'll kick you out. After a few of those, they behave.

When you're in the bathroom and she's talking to you, say, "I'm sorry, I'm going to have to talk to you later about this." If she responds with something like "Really quick though, I just want to . . ," cut her off and repeat, "I have to talk to you in about five minutes. Sorry, honey."

Or you can try what Keith does when I try to talk to him while he's in the bathroom: Respond with mouth fart noises like it's a language. Responding to something that turns you off with something that turns her off is a guaranteed winner.

I don't think my boyfriend washes his hands after he uses the bathroom. I am so grossed out by that thought that it's affecting our physical relationship. I don't know how to bring this up, but I feel like I have to. How do you tell someone something like this?

There was this Oprah special that someone told me about where she sent people into a woman's filthy house to clean it up and teach her lessons about her dirty ways. When checking her computer in a lab, they found fecal particles on the keyboard. After hearing that, I never wanted to scrub my hands more after using the bathroom. Find something like that story on the Internet and print it out. Make sure it's from a reputable source, like CNN. Pass it to your boyfriend as if the information shocked you as well. If he doesn't change his ways after reading that, then thank your god of choice that you have not married the idiot yet.

Call him cute names like "Shitty" and "Ol' Shit-Hands" until he gets it. What is it about the bathroom that is so taboo? I'd think that these would be the easiest hang-ups to solve. Wash off your disgusting poo-nail, or you can't touch me. The End. He's just not realizing how gross it is, but once you spell it out he has to agree. There's no way Crap Fingers can have an intelligent rebuttal.

"Well, if anything, my hands are dirtier than my dick, so after I pee I guess I should be washing my *dick* after I take a piss."

Fine, then wash your dick when you're done too. Take a shower. We don't care. Just clean up, and quit expecting us to listen to the science and hygiene facts that you took from an old comedy album.

My husband likes to crank the air conditioner in the bedroom before we go to sleep. I end up freezing if it's kept on, but he ends up in a sweat if it's not completely blasted. Is there a solution for this?

It sounds unromantic, but having your own blanket could be the solution. I know that everyone thinks of lovers sleeping only in a spoon or other such tangled and idealistic positions, but when it comes to actual sleep, you need to be more realistic.

Have the air cranked for your husband and add however many blankets on your side of the bed for you. Be loving and passionate, then say good night and sleep as if you're alone. Waking up not wanting to kill each other is one of the most romantic things a couple can do.

Chemda and I started our relationship with a queen-sized bed. It broke (wink), and then we went to my old twin bed. Without realizing it, we started sleeping in shifts due to lack of space. Eventually we got a king-sized bed. Our relationship has never been better. The space is necessary, and anyone who would doubt how good our relationship is, based on the fact that we sleep with space between us or facing away from each other, would be incredibly mistaken. You can't love another person if you can't rest every day, and you can only rest properly the way your body insists it rests properly. In fact, when I sleep, I don't like to be touched. I also don't care what a sleep scientist would say about that, because I know I'm in love and that I'm very, very comfortable.

My husband and I have a beautiful two-bedroom apartment to ourselves. However, one of the rooms is taken up with his junk. He's got things in there that he hasn't used in years. Some of the stuff can't even be reached because of the sheer volume of items in the room. I know he doesn't need this stuff, and I think it's unfair to take up an entire room for boxes of crap. He refuses to budge. Is a divorce over boxes in our future?

Yes, never-ending fights, no matter how petty, can lead to divorce. The subject matter ends up not being the source of contention; rather, the pain comes from feeling like your spouse doesn't listen or relate to you.

Pack rats don't respond very well to people telling them that their stuff is unnecessary. They believe that as soon as they throw something out, they will need that thing. Tell him why the clutter bothers you so much. Then tell him that you will work with him to help get this room to be more useful to both of you. Set one day a week where you both go through his stuff a bit at a time. He will become overwhelmed, defensive, and hurt, so you have to be the one to remain calm and patient. This may take a year and a couple therapy sessions, but it will be worth it in the end.

Start throwing shit out, a little bit each week. Pack rats don't know what they have. Save things like his dumb yearbooks, but trash things like beer signs with busted light bulbs. Replace your crap with most of his, and, if he complains, make him list the things he's missing. When he can't, tell him that he's welcome.

Or stage a robbery. When you guys go out, set up a friend to "break" into your house and only "steal" from your husband's bullshit memorabilia room.

"Wow honey, you were right. I guess you *did* have some nice shit. Oh well, time to move on."

My wife wakes up frequently during the night and is not subtle about it. She makes her way off the bed as if no one else is there. I often wake up and can't get back to sleep because of it. I know she can't help but need to use the bathroom, but do I have to wake up also?

I've thought that girls made noise deliberately at night so that you wake up and they have company. How can't they realize that at five A.M. a person doesn't bounce out of bed like it's a kiddie ride only to follow up with door slams behind them? You can't be nice when you try to stop this behavior. Every time it happens, say, "Are you doing this deliberately?" Act confused. "Why are you fucking with me? Are you mad at me?" It actually does get better. It won't stop, however, until you call her out a few times in a manner that makes her feel like an asshole and an idiot.

 Keith has told me that I wake him up when I open or close the door to the bedroom as well as when I get out of bed. He mentioned that he thought I was doing it on purpose. I, of course, wasn't. In fact, I always thought I was being subtle. I had to recognize that he's a very light sleeper and that I have to be more careful than I was being. The only way I knew that is because he made it a point to tell me. And tell me. And tell me again.

 I didn't write those last two sentences, but point taken.

My husband is thinking of getting rid of our home line. He claims that we don't need it since we both have cell phones. I want to agree with him, but it seems like not having a home phone line is odd. It feels like it makes the two of us separate in a way. Am I being too old-fashioned?

 I used to hate calling my girlfriend only to find that her husband picked up. I like the guy, but I know why I called, and it's not to make small talk with him until it's comfortable to ask to speak to my friend. I'm sure he didn't enjoy this chatter either.

You don't need a phone line for people to know that you're

together. Stop showing your age and wasting money on things that are no longer necessary. Give this one up. You won't miss it at all.

Quack quack, here comes Silly Goose.

First off, if you ever want to not answer your phone or act like you never got a message, it's easy to say you had cell phone problems. Everyone hates every phone carrier, and it's always believable that you not getting back to someone wasn't your fault. Second, when you want to get off the phone and you're using a cell phone, you can always say that you're getting onto the subway or that you're getting mugged. With a planted landline, everyone knows where you are. With today's superphones, there are applications that you can easily install that add background noise to your phone if you're done talking with the mother-in-law, such as car traffic or a baby crying. Dump the old phone, cavewoman. I can't think of one logical reason for your landline. Wait, what cool games does your landline have? See How We Can Get the Cord Tangled Around Us? Does it have that game? 'Cause mine has Missile Command.

My girlfriend is a slob. She wants me to move in with her, but I feel like her mess would drive me crazy and we would break up because of the fights I would have with her about silly things like putting away dishes. I love her and want to be closer, but have we reached the full potential of our relationship?

Is your girlfriend worth paying half the cost of a maid? Fuck it, she's the animal: Add the entire cost of a maid to the rent. You can get a nice immigrant very cheap. They won't understand the language, but they understand how to scrub a stove.

You're a smart man for thinking ahead instead of diving in and blaming her later for what you already knew. If your girlfriend really wants you to move in, then she has to do something about her mess. Tell her that if she can live mess-free on her own for a period of time that lets you see she can change, then you will know that she is serious about compromising and sharing her space with you. Just remember that even after she cleans up for a period of time, she's still a slobaholic at heart, and if she relapses, she agrees to pay the full price of Keith's maid.

My husband and I fell into the roles of me doing most of the cooking and him doing most of the dishes. Though we never officially declared these roles, we seem to prefer the ones we have over our partner's. I noticed, though, that my husband is starting to not make any effort to feed himself. He used to make sandwiches when I got busy or heat up a frozen meal here and again. Now, it seems even microwaving is a big ordeal. I know my role is cooking but I don't think that he should starve over it. Should I tell him to help himself when I'm not around or have I put myself in a position where I am solely responsible for his nutrition?

You have to take some of the blame for this, since you probably kept insisting on making the food your way or helping out even when you had other things to do. When you treat someone like a baby, they become one. Keep in mind that your husband won't actually die if you skip putting together a meal for him here and again. You might feel guilty the first few times, and he might eat the worst kind of food for him, but he'll be okay.

Yeah, I'll be okay. I guess . . .

My girlfriend and I have been living together for two years. I think it's working out fine until I look around and notice that she is still keeping her stuff separate from mine. Her DVDs are on a different shelf from mine, her board games aren't mixed in with any of my board games—that kind of thing. Is this a sign?

It's not necessarily a sign. Some people like their stuff separated because they like their things and they like having a sense of ownership. She also might have some form of OCD and that is how she likes to keep organized. The bigger deal is when you start buying things together. If she insists that she buys the couch and you buy the love seat, then you might have something to talk about.

I have this strange form of OCD. It means nothing. I just don't like to put Chemda's movies in with my collection. My collection was individually bought and thought out. Her shit was given to her as freebies or by friends. I don't want her copy of *Drop Dead Fred* (which is VHS, mind you; never mind we don't own a VHS player) next to my copies of *The Sixth Sense* and *The Matrix*. It'll make us look foolish.

And my games are so much better: Stratego, Connect Four, poker. . . . She wants to mix in Boggle and now the shelf is equally ours? Unfair. Simply unfair.

The Tao of Pooh she expects to be on the same shelf as Marilyn Manson's autobiography? She can't be serious.

A little behind-the-scenes: While writing this I looked up the trailer to *Drop Dead Fred*. I asked Chemda, "So this chick's just fucking insane? She's an adult that's spilling soup on herself in public? I need to feel for her?" Then Chemda started defending the movie. Sorry, but no one who thinks *Drop Dead Fred* is up there with *Tombstone* gets to share my shelf.

I usually buy the groceries for the house. I actually like going to the supermarket so that I can get exactly what I want. There have been times, however, when I can't make it in time to shop, so my husband goes instead. I don't know why, but he always buys the wrong things and adds unnecessary items to the list that we don't end up using.

My mother used to tell me that my dad did the same thing. She would do most of the shopping, and, on the rare occasion that he would go to the supermarket, he would buy the items that were packaged in the most pleasing, marketed, eye-catching manner. They also happened to be the most unnecessarily expensive versions of the food she needed. He would come home with little more than half the list right, and she would make do. Keith tends to do the same thing. I now get scared every time he goes to the market because I'm afraid that I'll end up with Emeril's Powdered Thyme instead of regular fresh thyme, rosemary instead of basil, and a BB gun instead of celery. I don't know why they behave this way, but sometimes I think it's so they never have to go to the store again. Keith?

My dad does the same thing that I do, so based on this page alone I think it's safe to say it's a guy thing. All three of us love our wives, and we're not trying to pull one over on anybody. We're just grocery retarded. I made a mistake the other day by buying peeled garlic instead of regular whole garlic. Why? I thought it'd be a nice treat. And Emeril's thyme that she's talking about said "*BAM!*" on it, real big and fun. Again, that's not a good surprise? When Emeril says, "*BAM!*," the whole audience goes crazy. Now think if you had that essence in your own kitchen!

I used to treat myself to this kind of shopping when I was struggling on food stamps. Instead of getting the generic ice cream for dessert, I took out my stamps and purchased a Viennetta. Us men don't have time to deal with all the intricate ins and outs of grocery stores. If it has gold lettering, they win.

It's not like we're trying to skirt the duty of grocery shopping—we just don't feel grocery shopping is an event. We don't have time, stores make our skin itch, and we're going to grab whatever's shiny.

My girlfriend has ten times the amount of clothing that I have. Why does she feel the need to take from my stash, and without asking to boot?

Sharing means caring?

We share so much that it seems okay to take Keith's clothes because they're handy, and I need them. Keith seems to not care what shirt he wears on any given day, so it's surprising to me when he gets annoyed when I borrow anything from him. I figure as long as it's not the last clean pair of undies, it's up for grabs.

For the record, you took the shorts that I wear when I'm out of undies, so, technically, it was the last pair of undies. But regardless . . .

Of course it's sexy when a girl wears her man's see-through white button-down shirt half opened around the house, and it's very hot when they wear their man's belt around their neck like a leash; however, ladies, we only have so many pairs of clothes, so don't offend us by just grabbing and wearing our stuff whenever you want. It's a pain when we throw on perfume-soaked clothes before we dash out. We're happy to buy you a top like the one you keep stealing from us. It wouldn't matter though. You'd still want *ours*.

Stop it, Chemda.

And you, this guy's girlfriend: Stop it.

I'm dumb?

Stop it.

Fighting

Through doing the KATG show, Keith and I discovered that women don't fight with their lovers. They "discuss" things or "disagree" with each other. I wish I could say that I've never succumbed to this brand of self-deluded craziness, but I have said (out loud and into a microphone) that Keith and I never fight. How could we? We love each other "the whole world!"

Well, good morning to me. Keith and I fight. How could we not? We spend more time with each other than with anyone else. We happen to work with each other as well as live together, so we have not only the relationship to fight about, but also the business.

You have to explain yourself more to the person you live with and love than to anyone else. For example, you can no longer just plan something on your own. If you want to see your friend on a Sunday, you have to make sure that someone didn't plan a surprise picnic for you on that day. If you need a vacation, you have to check with your partner to see about time, date, location, budget, mood, et cetera. Shit, if you even get up off the couch you're liable to get a "Where are you going?" That's all great when you first start dating someone. It feels incredible for someone to be so interested in you that they want to know where you are, where you're going, and how you felt while you were doing whatever it was you were doing. That said, I don't think Keith likes it when he comes home and I say something like "Our online bank statement told me that you *loved* the iPhone application store today. Yeah, Citibank told me that you loved it $143.89 much." And I certainly don't get excited when I have to discuss why I like to leave my clothing in the bathroom after I shower when there is a perfectly good hamper in the bedroom that would not take more than two seconds to use.

I'm always astonished that the phrases "Mind your own damn business," "Fucking leave me alone," and "Because I'm an asshole piece of shit who will never change, so deal with it already" are not exchanged between couples constantly. Is it LOVE that keeps us from snapping at each other? I know it's not love. It's restraint. It's the same muscle you use when you don't call your boss a dummy for pretending to know things just so he can keep his position. You were taught to do this when you were two years old. No one responds well to nasty, whiny, obnoxious tantrums. If you want someone to love you, you have to be lovable. That is not to say that you need to be okay with everything that your partner throws at you, but if you could stop rolling your eyes for a minute, you might get more credit as a human being.

Whatever she just wrote is right. She's always right. All hail the Queen.

FIGHTING Questions

Fighting with my wife never ends. She has brought up arguments that I thought were resolved months prior. How is this fair?

It's a bit hard to rationalize how we (as women) genuinely feel like an issue can be resolved—our curiosities about the topic fulfilled and the problem laid to rest—and then, months later: BOOM! It hits us again. I think what happens is that if a man does something that resembles the actions of the original issue, it triggers our initial feelings from before the problem was resolved. We feel like we were duped the first time into believing that things were okay.

So is it fair? I don't know. Is it fair that you did it again after I told you that it hurt me the last time you did it?! Wow. You really can't help yourself, can you?

You're feeling like you're having déjà vu, and she thinks the topic she's rehashing hasn't been resolved already. This is why I insist that arguments Chemda and I have are only discussed when we are on the air. This way there's always a record of it, and our listeners can remind Chemda how right I am. I believe she appreciates it.

First thing you'll need is a sound mixer. Something inexpensive and simple is fine. Get a few microphones—you don't want to have to share a mic during an argument—and download a cheap recording program you can understand.

If you don't have the time for this creative solution, calmly remind her how this argument was dealt with last time. Unfortunately, this means that you have to rehash the points and counterpoints that were originally made, but this time when the two of you reach a conclusion, take a minute to draw up a simple "We are not allowed to argue about [TOPIC OF DISCUSSION] anymore" contract, and have her sign it. If she insists on living in fights of the past, then there's no way the two of you will find time for exciting brand-new fights in the future.

My wife is disgusted by my lack of chivalry. I'm carrying all the bags! I can't open the door! I thought we were equals!

Sometime during your courting stage you did all the silly stuff for her. Every door was opened as if she was a cripple, her chair was pulled back and pushed in at restaurants, that kind of thing. (How stupid the chair-pulling-out one is. She really does the work. You're just standing there pretending to push the chair in like a doofus.) In all this stupidity, she got the idea that you'll always open a door for her and that you'll lay your coat down over puddles. Now that you don't, because it's not practical, she thinks it all means you take her for granted and that you're not in lust. Never mind that both hands are full and you're not a monkey. If you cared, you'd find a way.

You set the bar too high. You were fake in the beginning and now the real you doesn't stand a chance. You have to kill her.

Your wife has an idea in her head of what a man should be. It's one of those things that relates to the fairy tales that we were exposed to. The good news is that you're probably a nice guy, because you actually care what she's bitching about. The bad news is that in order to maintain sanity and order, you will have to pander a bit to the princess brain. So, when your hands are full of groceries and you can't be the one to open the door, mention that you wish you had a third hand so that she would never ever have to lift one, because you love her so much.

Are we equals? Yes. You cover for her when she needs to be a princess and she will tell the tales far and wide of how you slayed all the dragons, you big strong knight, you.

I've heard that you shouldn't go to bed angry, but sometimes you have to go to sleep because there's work the next day. Right?

Yes, right. This was Chemda's idea when we got serious in our relationship. It sounded nice. But then some days it didn't make sense. Not all arguments can be solved in a day, let alone by bedtime. You can agree to discuss things civilly, but despite Chemda's answer to the last question, we really don't live in a fairy-tale world, and our coach won't turn into a pumpkin at the stroke of midnight. It's okay if we sleep a little upset, rest, and try to come at the person a little calmer and more focused the next day. We're adults. It's okay to go to bed huffy if you're not being spiteful. If this affected sex, then whoever you later decide was more wrong owes the other person oral.

Keith is right. I really thought that we should stay up and resolve problems, because I felt like issues grow when they are not tended to right away. It's hard to stop an argument midway. You have to somehow not respond to something that you are extremely passionate about, take a step back, and calm down enough to fall asleep. The truth is, though, that you probably have both said every point you have on the matter and are now going in circles. The more time that passes, the more tired you are, and the more likely you are to stop listening to one another. In order to reassure the other that the matter will not end just because it's bedtime, come up with a tactic for the next day. Promise each other that, instead of verbally rehashing everything, you'll each write down your side and what you think the other person's view is. This way, you can rest knowing that you will be heard. Also, try to not make the argument the last thing that you talk about. Find a better part of the day and discuss that so that the night can end on a sweet note.

My boyfriend and I have to commute together, but we get very cranky in the car. How do we make for a more peaceful ride?

I hear ya, sister. Even Chemda and I had this problem. "Gasp, even *you!*" Yep. I'm tall, my legs hurt being squooshed, I feel like I have to keep Chemda entertained because she usually drives, traveling makes her cranky, she's not amused by my antics, and by the time we're at our destination we want to kill ourselves. Then one day we realized that it's okay if we're not always talking like we would at a dinner or another event where it's just us. We'll have fun when we get to where we're going; we don't need to push it. I bring a book, a magazine, or some music, like I'm a child, and she zones out about what blended spreads she's going to make at our next house party. Everybody wins, and we arrive at our destination intact. Now, maybe you're thinking, "Is it safe that Chemda zones out while she's driving?" Hey, I'm not gonna tell her . . .

The zoning-out thing that I do is to escape Keith when he thinks that singing his own lyrics to every song that he plays is both hilarious and romantic. Amazingly, zoning out makes me less likely to crash than listening to Keith's version of "Welcome to the Jungle." Leave each other alone in the car if engaging isn't working. You're not a bad couple. You're just collecting more things to talk about once you reach your destination.

My wife and I argue every Valentine's Day, anniversary, birthday, et cetera. I feel like her expectations are always so high that one detail out of place throws her off. I get that these days are special, and I try my best, but it's never good enough. How can I get her to relax?

You can't. You just can't. It's seriously that simple. You can't win with some people. I would love to celebrate Valentine's Day with Chemda. But she always feels unnecessary pressure for the day to be perfect. So now we get nothing. Oh well. I guess I save money and time. Shrug.

"Valentine's Day is a crock," she'll say. "If you love someone, then love them every day."

"Okay, how about today?"

"Fuck that shit!"

Aye yie yeesh . . .

Valentine's Day is a made-up holiday that I don't celebrate because I *know* I will be disappointed. It's too much pressure, and everyone is trying to outdo the next couple. I can't fault people for caring about the day, though, because I know that, for me, my birthday is one of the highlights of my year, and I will admit that I really need to feel special on that day (and the days surrounding). I do, however, get disappointed easily by these celebrations. My hope is that everyone will get along, my partner will be doting over me the entire day, and no one will be tired until I get sleepy so that I can have the company I want for as long as I want it. The truth is that not all of my friends get along with each other, so putting them in the same room to celebrate is a bust. My partner has to still be human and take a minute to himself here and again throughout the day, and people get tired. Where does that leave me? I try to be as involved with the planning as I can so that I keep all these things in mind, but something fails every year. Keith is right. You can't win. No one can. Keep getting excited, though. I just *know* this year is the one!

My wife fights with me whenever I disagree with her opinions. We can't possibly have the same thoughts all the time. Am I screwed?

Yep, pretty much. Maybe she needs to be with somebody who really does agree with everything and see how horrible that would be. Or maybe she thinks you disagreeing with her makes her look stupid. Maybe with her it's all about being the best couple at the dance, and if you two disagree in public on what actor played the best James Bond, then there's no way people will think you're the King and Queen.

I say look up her arguments and come back at her with facts. If, for example, she really does think that Roger Moore was a better James Bond than Sean Connery, why not find out the truth? When doing a simple search online, I found that Sean Connery is loved over 40 percent more than any other James Bond actor. You can't argue with Internet facts.

My husband throws things around when he gets mad. I don't see why he would want to destroy things that belong to us. How do I get him to stop?

I understand the urge to break things. The great Fred Durst said it best when he sang, "Damn right I'm a maniac." I'll bang the desk like a monkey when I get mad. Now I'm trying to do it less in my girl's presence, but I can't help it sometimes. That's not an excuse. I need to learn. I may not stop hitting things like a child, but I can learn not to do it in front of witnesses.

Your man sounds more extreme, but I understand. If he's not throwing these things at your head or yelling at you as he does it, it's normal. We're still cave idiots, and if money and space aren't issues, he needs a section of the garage where he's allowed to break things. He needs a section away from you where he can hammer a piece of wood simply in the name of frustration. If a garage isn't possible, turn the other way when he goes out into the yard with a sledgehammer. We're men. You like that we have man in us.

Unfortunately it comes with silliness like this. In fact, truth to tell, it's healthier to break shit and move on than it is to hold things in and let them fester like women do. It was a cheap Martha Stewart Kmart clock! I'm *soooo* sorry I broke it . . . I'm sure it was worth *millions* . . .

As natural as it is to want to throw everything out the window when you're angry, you can't just respond however you like all the time. If we did, we would punch the person who took our cab when we knew it was our turn, and we would yell at the person next to us on our commute about personal hygiene. We all have to behave. However, here is your opportunity to have fun with your husband. Next time you get mad, light something on fire and blame it on human instinct. Then head over to couples therapy, because clearly you both need help.

When we plan dinner outings, my girlfriend always asks me where I want to eat. My answer is always that I don't care (because I don't), but she insists that I make a suggestion. I don't know why I bother suggesting anything, because she vetoes all of my ideas until I pick a place that she wants to go to. Why can't she just start off by saying she wants to go there instead of this silly exchange that always ends up in an argument?

Every girl is like this. They pick on us men for being so indecisive about things, but meanwhile we really don't care. And the thing is: You, the lady, *do* care. You care what we eat or where we go. Men don't. Wherever we pick will probably be wrong. Wherever you pick will definitely be right. Not caring if we have pasta or tuna doesn't mean we don't care about you.

Are you picking stupid places? Maybe she's vetoing your choices because you've been to the places that you're suggesting, you hated them, and you can't even remember that. Making suggestions to where you both will be going out is considerate. Shrugging when someone asks you to help is asinine and infuriating. If they asked you at work if you liked one project over another, would you shrug and tell them you don't care? Or would you show interest and express a real response? Can you even answer *these* questions, or are you still shrugging?

I don't like my girlfriend's friends. Is this going to be an issue?

Yes, this will be an issue. These girls will most likely be around forever. I say, when you're out with your girlfriend and her friends, find the other boyfriends and hang out with them. Most likely, they are in the same position and just want to drink and stay away from your girlfriend just like you do theirs.

Be careful; friends can be a reflection of who she is. If all her friends look like clones of each other, then you're dating one of the replicas. If that is the case, then run.

My fiancée won't let me go to strip clubs. Is it worth making it a big deal, or should I just let it go?

Should you just let it go? Sure. And who needs dessert with dinner? You don't *need* it. So let it go.

Not letting you do stuff was your mother's job.

How important is it for you to go to strip clubs? Will you eventually end up lying about going? If this is something that you need to do, then she needs to be okay with it or you both will have a problem with it during your entire relationship.

Tell your girl, "Look, I'm not going to the Champagne Room, and I'm not spending cash we can't afford. I'm going to the strip club tonight. You want ten new pairs of shoes? Is that what you spend your money on? Fine. I don't care. But wait, why do you need those shoes? Your New Balance tennies are fine with me. Who are you trying to attract in your Blahniks, whore?"

Waahhh! I can't go to the strip club! Waahhh!

My man wants to have Guys' Night Out. Why can't it just be us? Or why can't I come along? What shadiness really goes on?

This ties in with the previous question. Guys need to decompress here and again or they'll burst like a refining plant. When we go on our guys' nights out we might drink a little too much or badmouth chicks, but we're not cheating on you. In fact, it's *not* being allowed to go out that will cause infidelity, and that's because we've snapped. Guys will all of a sudden think about what they can and cannot do, and go crazy. "I can do whatever I want!" Give them a night at the bar or a strip club once a while and you're actually having more control over them, not less.

Why do you want to go everywhere with your boyfriend? Do you want to go to work with him as well? Might as well. I'm sure he's having a blast without you. In fact, what is he doing while you read this book? Oh my God! Quick! Go check!

What's wrong with you? Do you want him to tag along every time you go out with your girlfriends? Are you making out with someone every time he turns around? Give him his space or he'll resent you.

Last week my wife and I were at a baby shower. I said an off-the-cuff remark that she was not pleased with. No one heard what I said, and I apologized for it right away, but it was too late. The comment had set her off, and she was seeing red. I asked if we could discuss the problem when we got home because there were so many people around, but my wife refused. She does this very often. This behavior embarrasses me to no end. Am I wrong to think that we should hold off a fight for when we are in private, or am I being insensitive?

It's funny—not funny ha-ha, but funny fuckin' ridiculous—that a lot of women think that after they were treated insensitively by their man that they must get some *mea culpa* right there and then, no matter who is watching. They take private things, and, as far as I can see, they make the whole thing even worse by making it public. Yes, some things—in fact, most things—can wait. The man is trying to stop any more embarrassment from being caused, and the woman seems to want to bring more on. Will she feel better after her man grovels in public about something everyone is out of the loop about?

 Keith has told me in the past that he has been embarrassed because I raised my voice in public. To be honest, I wasn't even aware that other people could hear me or that they were looking in our direction at all. I was probably feeling rejected or neglected, and I needed to make sure I was heard. Of course my timing could have been better, but I also think that a little emotional support from Keith would have made things easier.

When your wife is nowhere near angry and you two are alone, tell her how her freaking out in public makes you feel, then ask her if there is any way to make the matter not escalate when she does become angry at you around others. Now you're putting some of the responsibility on her. By having this conversation when she's not angry, you have a chance to get a clearer explanation about what you did wrong, and she has a chance to really notice the impact of her behavior.

Every time we have a fight, my girlfriend cries at some point. I get that girls are very sensitive, but I feel like when she starts with the waterworks it throws everything off balance. I suddenly can't hold my case right because I feel bad for her. I think this allows her to get away with a lot and it stifles me from telling my side. How can I not let the crying affect my strength to fight?

This question is impossible. The problem is that some women really do use crying as a weapon—a fact that makes my following statement, though true, a bit harder to swallow. Real crying is just another expression of emotion. My crying doesn't mean you have to stop and "save" me before we continue what we're discussing. To women, crying does not mean we're broken. It's just an outward appearance of some sadness that, if we're fighting, I assume you're feeling too (despite your lack of tears, Robot).

If you're male, everything I just wrote makes no sense to you. I can describe crying in whatever way I want, but it's no use. To men, crying equals death, and nothing will ever change that.

How little credit they give us. . . . Here's the deal: I learned that girls can't help crying, because they are so passionate about what they're feeling. (What assholes us men must look like for never crying. *"If you really cared you'd be crying like me!"*) As a man, it is absurd to me that girls don't understand how manipulative this is, whether it's intentional or not. What I've also learned is shocking but the truth: You have to ignore the tears. You have to talk to these things as though they aren't crying, and if that seems to make the waterworks flow harder, you have to ignore that, too. Once you can control your reaction to their tears, you've also protected yourself against women who *do* manipulate with tears— their Kryptonite will no longer have an effect on you.

When my husband gets upset, he gets quiet and wants to be left alone. I respect this about him, and I give him his space, but because he distances himself from the issue we end up never talking about what happened. Because of this I feel that the

issue never gets resolved. **How can I get my husband to talk about what he has issues with during fights?**

The irony is that when you confront him about this, he'll get upset and have to leave.

Sorry, but you tell him Uncle Keith says he has to grow up and be a man. Time by yourself after an argument is fine, but he's not even taking a break and coming back. He thinks this is the end of it. He needs to grow up and quit acting like a girl. (No offense.)

I say when he leaves to sulk, you start blowing his friends. Word will get back to him, and he won't leave so fast during discussions.

I think it's really smart to give a person some space when they request it. However, not coming back to the issue is dangerous. How about while he's taking his time out, you take the time to write out what you would be expressing to him if he were in the room with you? Then, when he's had time, pass the letter along to him and ask him to respond, whether it be verbal or written. This way he gets his space, but you also get what you need.

My husband and I get along great. We like to socialize together all the time. We go out, host dinner parties at our place, or go to our friends' places very often. Our problem tends to begin when we both drink enough to get drunk. We both behave more defensively, and we end up fighting over nothing. It's easy to just tell us not to drink, but drinking is a huge part of social situations as adults. How can we drink with each other and not have it lead to a petty fight?

Are you serious? You're telling me that excessive drinking is ruining your relationship and asking me what you should do about it? If you can't stop yourself from drinking to a point of developing contempt for each other, you need AA. Drinking is very much a part of adult life, but you should have control over your intake-to-bitch ratio at this point. How far will you push each other to learn this lesson? Grow up.

Drink from the right side of your mouth only. That side affects the left side of your brain. It is the right side that becomes defensive. You two idiots should be fine.

Or, try meth.

My husband has developed a bad habit of responding at home to his bad day at work. If he had a bad time with some people at work, he will come home and let it out on me. He yells at anything I do, and he is generally difficult to be around. He says that I should understand and try to stay out of his way, but he's too hard to avoid, and it's my house that I would be hiding in. What should I do about this behavior?

Your husband is wrong. Dead wrong. Tell him that while you drag your thumb slowly across your neck.

When people lose their temper they are not in their right mind, and they are too difficult to reason with. Approach your husband when he is not upset. Tell him how his behavior scares and upsets you. Make sure that he knows that you are on his side by being very calm and nurturing.

Offer solutions: When he gets home knowing that he's had a bad day, he should let you know right away and place himself alone with things that make him feel better, like TV, a radio, the computer, games, et cetera. After having about a half hour or so (he might need more in the beginning), he can come out of the room and try talking to you about what went wrong. After practicing this, he will become more familiar with his temper and be able to control his emotions more carefully.

 Wow, what a fuckin' douche your husband is. You're being abused. This is not okay. You need out. I recommend you watch the Jennifer Lopez tour-de-force *Enough*. She gets abused in that movie just like you. Study it, and the next time your man knocks you to the ground with words, lie there, seemingly helpless. He'll go for one last insult while you're on the ground. That's what cowards do. When he leans in to verbally assault you that final time, that's when you strike.

I'd tell you more, but I'm not your accomplice. I'm just a friend.

My husband and I get into a fight every time we get lost while driving. We both think we know it all, and we refuse to ask anyone for help. We end up tacking on a huge amount of time to our drive and showing up to our destination angry with each other. How can we avoid behaving like this when both of us are so stubborn?

 Get a GPS unit. The driver's in charge of it.

Keith is right. Get a GPS system. Take turns driving. The driver will be the only person to navigate. If the driver gets lost despite having the navigational system, there will be no "I told you so"s, and no "I knew it"s. Be on each other's side, and calm the fuck down.

One of my husband's and my pastimes at home is watching TV. When we find ourselves wanting to watch different things at the same time, it always starts a fight. We both hate each other's programs, and we both think that the other should be the one to compromise. What can we do about this?

1)   Don't have kids. Not being able to get the TV time that you want is a nine-year-old child's biggest problem with his sister. The fact that two adults are having such a big issue about it is a bit retarded.

2)   Get other hobbies. TV seems to be rotting your brain.

3)   Learn to share. Take turns with the TV. Most programs are half an hour to an hour long. If you each only get one hour with the TV, you can switch off and manage to save brain cells at the same time.

Flip a coin. The winner watches what they want, and the other person records their show for later. Jesus . . .

When we fight, my wife gets so mad that sometimes she physically pushes me. I always end up walking away because I can't think of another response to her behavior. Nothing ends up

getting resolved when this happens. What can I possibly do about this?

Your wife is fighting you because she ran out of words to express how she is feeling. Resorting to violence is unacceptable and should not be tolerated. Your wife needs to learn how to communicate how she feels, no matter how hard it is. When she starts pushing you, don't be so passive as to walk out of the room. Tell her very sternly to stop. Insist that she tell you, in words, what she's going through. Even if she expresses her frustration without keeping on the subject matter, this will help the situation. If she stops and tells you what's wrong, you and she can realize what's happening to her and you will be able to get back to the original problem and figure it out more calmly. If she does not stop, then walk away. However, know that once she calms down, you are responsible for bringing up the issue that you were arguing about in the first place. If you do not bring it up, you are letting her get away with hitting you as a means to resolving a fight.

Push her back. Not too hard, but enough for her to remember that you can physically crush her at a moment's notice. Act confused as to why the push shocked her so much.

"So pushing's unacceptable? Okay. Now I know that it's better to talk like adults."

And then run. You are about to be arrested. That's how life works. You can't push your wife. Cops won't care that you were pushed first.

And when the cops come, if they give you a hassle, give them a little shove also. Not too hard, just enough to show that you deserve respect.

My wife and I wake up at the same time for work every morning. She is a morning person and knows that I'm not. So why does she insist on trying to chat every morning? It's hard for me to think, and I end up responding wrong or not at all because I'm not fully awake yet. If she knows I'm not myself, why does she insist on the behavior that will lead to a fight?

Damn if I know . . . These women make all our schedules and plans; they can tell what we're thinking by the look on our face, and they're incredibly intuitive; yet, somehow they have no idea that we're about to pass the fuck out or we just came from a dream where our mom was a unicorn on Volcron 7 and nothing makes sense to us yet. I think they do it because we don't challenge them on anything they say when we're dog tired, and if we technically agree to something they're sneaking into a conversation like a shady lawyer, it still counts.

If I'm not ready to talk, a woman gets nothing out of me. I won't be tricked. It either leads to me agreeing to something I won't like, or we get into a fight where there's no way I can win. Just keep the trap shut. The only business I do lying down is monkey business.

If you're the passive-aggressive type, try this: Morning people are usually terrible at night. Wait until she's very tired and talk to her about something that is really important to you. See if she can keep up. If she doesn't learn from that, buy something that you know she normally wouldn't approve of, and when she goes to yell at you, tell her that she said it was okay the other night. She will say something like "You know I'm no good at night." Smile that retarded grin she hates. She'll get it for sure.

 No one is trying to take advantage of you. She's just not empathizing with you not being a morning person. She's only thinking about what is going through her own head. I agree with Keith. Don't answer. Tell her you can't focus, and that you two need to talk about whatever it is later.

The Body
(Outer Beauty)

"Keith, are you a breast man or an ass man?"

"Yep."

I love the female body so much. I'm not an eye guy or a lips guy or a tits guy or an ass guy. I'm just a guy. And I love it all. Smart unattractive chicks love picking on attractive girls, citing how smart they are and how dumb models are.

"Models are dumb, and stupid. Supermodel? Yeah, right. More like super *dumb!*"

Thank you, Janeane Garofalo.

Thing is, you're born with your intelligence. For the most part you can't control things like common sense. You can take a class or four, but throughout my life I've never seen someone I know improve or decrease their overall smarts. I have, however, seen many people lose weight and look better. So here's what I propose: Instead of smart people bragging about how much smarter they are than good-looking people, they keep their jealousy to themselves and start realizing that keeping hot and fit is harder than staying smart. I've read a book or two in my day— chips on my lap, beer in my hand. It wasn't hard. I've also been on the gym's dreadmill. Guess which one was harder work? And guess which one is more useful in the long term? Sure, I can't begin to tell you how many times $E = mc^2$ has helped me day to day, but staying attractive is much more work. And, quite frankly, attractiveness is what we first care about in a mate.

Not *you*. I know you're much better than that. You go for mind and soul and blah blah bullshit.

Liar.

"I'm not shallow. The first thing I notice is the brain. It's the most attractive organ."

Is it? You saw that with your X-ray glasses? Look, we can't help you if you're not going to be honest with us. Why are you lying to a book? Who's the book going to tell? You think when the bookstore closes this book and *Men Are from Mars* are going to laugh about your shallowness? Grow up.

Of course the body is the first thing we all notice. You're not sad to think that way. It's impossible for it to be any way else. A man or woman can work around body deficiencies with wit and charm, but your judgment on them started at first sight. And rightfully so. Nothing you can do about it.

The problem with us—and this includes women—is that we let a lot of issues go when the person has a hot body. More often than not, we don't hold on to a person with a good personality if the looks aren't there. Many people will think this is unfair. I say nay. If you stop talking and sharing your personality, your personality is no longer there. Your body is always there. For better or for worse, you can't hide your body by shutting up. You can "cleverly" add another layer of clothing, but we all know your tricks, and we can safely guess what's underneath. That's another reason I like girls in skimpy clothing: I don't have to guess what she really looks like. Skinny, fat—now I know. That's out of the way, and we can move on to Kierkegaard.

What am I saying? I'm saying that it's time to do a few crunches, Pig. Grilled chicken isn't your enemy.

THE BODY (OUTER BEAUTY) Questions

How do I tell my girlfriend that I think she needs to douche?

Next time you're messing around and it starts getting hot and heavy, put a finger or two of yours in her vagina and then put it in her mouth. She may not admit that she doesn't like it because she doesn't want to ruin the mood or be embarrassed, but after sex it will become a priority in her world to take care of that mess.

If she can't keep her downstairs clean, she's going to get fewer visitors there. Show her how much more you're into it when it's fresh from the cleaner's.

A lot of women like to throw out how douching rids the body of important vitamins and whatnot. Some hippie told them that they'll get cervical cancer by even *looking* at a douche bottle. Everyone's a doctor all of a sudden. A douche now and again wouldn't kill you, honey. Douching will ruin your body's delicate balance? Well, your balance stinks.

Women don't necessarily *have* to douche, but you do have to keep clean. Women need to remember this: The pussy is an armpit with a hole.

I smell myself sometimes. Everything on my body that's dark and damp—armpits, belly button, balls—develops an odor. It's the exact same odor that forms in a pussy. It's the smell of murky and dank. These areas need to be showered after exercise or things of that nature. It's normal, and it needs to be recognized.

One more time: Your pussy is an armpit with a hole. It's the thing most likely to stink on the body besides the asshole. Women need to recognize it and understand that it's a personal affront to their partner if it hasn't been cleaned.

Leave this book open in the bathroom to this page for her to find.

If you're the woman reading this, your man didn't deliberately leave this page open for you (even though earlier he tried to make you taste yourself), but what a great coincidence it *was* left on this page! Now you know!

I'm afraid that my penis is too small. How can I get over that?

If your penis is small, start learning more things than you think you need to know about a woman. Learn everything about what pleases a vagina. Be Edward Penishands. Be the King of the Pussy Eaters. And while you're at it, make a lot of money. Money makes your penis grow.

Everybody thinks their penis is too small. Besides that though, remember that there's someone for everyone. (Look around. I'm not making this shit up.) Howard Stern's infamous for exclaiming on rooftops about the lack of manhood he holds, and (as of press time) he's married to a model. (And there are plenty of dudes with money she could be fucking.) There's a girl out there looking for a corkscrew-looking penis. Another's looking for all bent and fucked up. Don't bring this up ahead of time—there's no reason—but, like every other guy, you bring your bag of what you think are problems to a relationship and the other person decides what they like and don't like.

Alternatively, you can just date Asians.

Plus it's easy for you to tuck in and reenact that scene from *The Silence of the Lambs*. Everyone gets a chuckle out of that.

Really, every guy thinks his penis is small? You guys are weird.

This guy I'm seeing may be the last man on earth who doesn't trim his pubic hair. How can I bring up this subject?

Men in general take things much better than women. When it comes to grooming, men *want* to be told. For example, I always thought ankle socks were for chicks and queers. Nope. Most women prefer that look to socks that go past the ankle. I never knew. Now I know, and I can see how girls on the street want me. For that, I thank my lady. Same with pubes. A girl told me, I thanked her, I trimmed, and The Monster has never looked better. Chicks dig it, and on a hot summer's day my balls smell less like bad pussy.

This one's easy. Just tell him. He wants to know.

Tell him his penis will look and feel at least an inch bigger. That gets men to do anything.

My girlfriend is talking about getting a boob job. I think her breasts are just fine. How can I convince her not to do it?

It is really hard to change a person's own self-image. More than likely the decision to get a breast job has been brewing way before you even came along. There's a certain way that we look at ourselves that becomes ingrained and stubbornly stays in our psyche regardless, sometimes, of contradicting facts. The best thing you can do is encourage her by telling her how beautiful all her body parts are, including her chest. It may help her to hear and feel a positive point of view on a regular basis. You may also want to do some research about breast augmentation so that you can bring her some facts about the procedure.

Why do big boobs scare you so much? Let her make her own decisions. She gets to have what she's always wanted, and you get to be with a chick with killer knockers. Johnny Tit-Hater over here . . .

I'm twenty-seven, and I believe that I have been dating the perfect person for me. I can see spending the rest of my life with her except for one snag. I am normally into very big-chested women, and she has almost no breasts. Is it wrong to ask her to get a boob job? I feel like this will make everything perfect.

I can't imagine anyone telling me that I'm perfect in every way, but I just need to get a boob job or a nose job or any other job. I would just always be self-conscious about what else you thought you wanted to change about me physically. However, people take plastic surgery so much more lightly than they used to. It's very possible that your girl has been thinking about getting one and you just don't know it. Either way, this will obviously be an issue for you unless it's done, so why not express it? Here's how you do it: Test the waters about how she feels about other girls getting breast jobs by watching movies or looking through magazines. Express how you think it's great that modern technology has improved so much that fake boobs look and feel so real that you can't even tell the difference. Then mention that you know some girls who changed their lives for the better by getting the operation. If she's feeling open and at ease at that point, joke around about how you would pay for the left one for the opportunity to name it. Soon you'll be laughing about it and before you know it, your perfect girl is beside you. Now, if only she just took care of that little ear thing she's got going on . . . Am I right?

I met your chick. *That's* your only hang-up? Hey, different strokes . . .

I slept with my new girlfriend of three months quite a few times and never saw her topless. Why does she refuse to remove her shirt and how can I get her to feel comfortable?

Because her last boyfriend made her get a boob job and that ended up not being enough for him so he dumped her and now she's very self-conscious about her chest.

THIS JUST IN: Chicks are weird. Her hang-up is her breasts, whether they're scarred or spectacular.

Tell her how much you love her, how sexy it would be to see her tits, how it's cruel that she keeps that from you, and see what happens. In fact, I say go so far as to covering up your balls. When she says how weird that is, look back at her and say, *"Durrr . . ."*

I could be wrong, though. Maybe the hang-up is that she's fat. Let her know that you already know that she's fat and that vertical stripes can only do so much.

Your girlfriend is not comfortable with herself. Go slow. Every time you fool around make sure she knows how much you like her body. Go for some spots that are covered just a little more every time. Keep the lights off at first so that she doesn't feel like there's a spotlight on her. If none of that works, then maybe you should take the hint. She's saving *you* from what's under there. Leave it alone.

I am a twenty-year-old male. My scrawny physique prevents me from having the confidence to hit on women. I tried bulking up but it seems that this is the body that I'm stuck with. Am I destined to be alone?

You don't have to be huge for a girl to really like you. In fact, some women prefer a skinny guy. Also, if you're trim, you'll be able to get ripped a lot faster. Working out is always a good idea. Being in shape is hot no matter what body type you are.

I was bone scrawny up until my senior year in high school. You could see the spine in my back. Then it all changed, so you're not necessarily stuck with your physique for life. But let's assume you are. Guess what? Now's the time for that look. Girls like their boys to look skinny and emaciated. It's the new thing. I don't know how it happened, but girls don't want a guy who can help move their TV across the room anymore. They want someone they can arm wrestle and defeat. Look at the bands topping the charts. Look at the "men" in fashion magazines.

Nerds are the new cool, and skinny is the new sexy. I don't like it, but it works for you. Enjoy.

My girlfriend is getting fat. I don't want to be a jerk, but I'm losing my attraction toward her. I don't want to lose her. Is there a gentle way to bring up weight issues with women?

No, there is no gentle way to bring up weight with a woman. However, there is a way to get her back on track. If you are a man who already works out, then invite her to work out with you. Make it sound like a great thing that you guys can do together. Make her feel like you want to include her in more of your routines. If you're not a man who works out, then let her know that you've been thinking about starting a routine and that you're hoping that, as encouragement to you, she would be your partner. If you go out to eat a lot together, make better choices in your restaurant, choose lighter meals, or do something active on your dates instead of just going out to eat. All these things will seem more romantic. The result is a healthier, fitter girlfriend, and you have brownie points to boot.

Make sure she doesn't eat those brownies. And stop getting her chocolate when you fuck up. Flowers are not edible.

I recently broke up with someone. During our three years of dating I gained fifty pounds. Now that I'm on my own and with

this weight, my confidence has gone way down mainly because I feel fat. How do I get back in the game?

Hmmm . . . Damn . . . I guess we don't have all the answers. Lemme think . . . Think, Me, think . . . I sure hope we don't have to give our book advance money back for not being able to come up with an answer. Shit, shit, shit. My dad was right: Who am I to think I could write a book? Damn . . .

Wait! I got it! Quit shoving food down your fuckin' piehole! Whew . . . that was close . . .

You get back in the game by eating less and exercising. Confidence should only happen to those who earn it. You enjoyed eating and didn't get to go out on dates; others enjoyed fucking but couldn't eat all the cake they wanted.

Lose weight, get confidence, and quit writing stupid fuckin' questions.

Obviously, you want to lose weight. You also don't want to feel alone for too long because that will get you out of the social habit. What you can do to boost both your physical and mental health is join a couple of groups that focus on exercising and weight loss. This will put you in a place where people not only share a great common goal, but they will also be easily relatable, and you will feel less judged. You should also think of your ex every time you want to eat something you know you're not supposed to.

I've been dating a man for a few months now and everything is going great. However, recently I saw some pictures of his ex-girlfriends and noticed that their physical traits are common to each other and completely different from mine. Is it normal that I'm kind of freaked out?

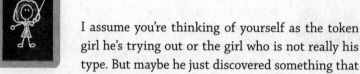

Yes, it's normal you're freaked out; however, it's not rational.

Maybe he grew up and realized he likes something new. Whatever. Don't even ask questions. You're not in a movie where he's dating you as a bet. And even if he was, he'll realize at the end that it was you he loved all along.

I assume you're thinking of yourself as the token girl he's trying out or the girl who is not really his type. But maybe he just discovered something that wasn't in his path before. If he's with you, you turned his head enough for him to want to be with you for a while. Think of it this way: Other than their looks, you know what else these girls have in common? They're all no longer with your man. *Snaps!*

I started dating my girl because she's different from other women I've met. She's more open-minded, intelligent, and fun than other people I've met in general. When we first met, she had a couple of tattoos and a navel piercing. Now, after a year of us being together, she has two more tattoos and three more piercings. My fear is that I don't see an end to the decorations, and the piercings are starting to seem more like body mutilations. To me, it seems like she's getting carried away. Am I a prude? Can I get her to stop? What can I do to make my girl-friend stop inking and puncturing her skin?

You claim that a huge part of why you like her is because she is open and into new things, but you want to be the one to tell her when her openness has reached its max? If you're not into what she's interested in doing to her body, then you may not actually be attracted to who she is. She may just inspire you more as a friend than a girlfriend.

Is she so open-minded and intelligent that if you question what she's doing with her body you're a square and an oppressor? It sounds like you love the idea of her free spirit, but you don't like the fact that you might see her tongue cut in half like a lizard tomorrow morning.

Bring it up to her. If she immediately calls you the Man Devil that's holding her back, she's one of the not-fun female renegades. If, however, she's open to what you're saying, sit her down to talk about what Daddy did to her. Maybe your chat will help calm some demons and teach her that pain doesn't always equal love.

My girlfriend recently gained a bit of weight. It's nothing major, and she's not fat in any way, but it seems like she might not have noticed that she is not the same size. Everything she wears is now just a bit too small for her and it looks ridiculous. How can I tell a girl I love that her pants are causing that muffin-top effect to her body?

The waist is a very sexy part of a female. Putting a hand on a woman's waist can spark up sensual feelings not just for the person touching it but for the person being touched as well. That being said, start making a habit of grabbing her muffin top. Every now and again squeeze it a little for extra insurance. This does not feel good and should cause her to look into changing it.

First, be honest. Having a muffin top is fat in *some* way. Now that we're honest with what needs to be done, we can get down and dirty. Chemda's dead on. In order to point out fat anywhere on the body, give that part of the body extra attention. When you're lying next to each other, throw it an extra jiggle. Don't cave and say you love it. Just fiddle with it like you're messing with your hair or picking at your nails.

I'm not big on manipulation, but she tricked you by starting to become a pig. It's okay to trick back to make her good again.

My husband refuses to get properly dressed for company. He thinks that since guests are coming over to his house, he can put on whatever he feels like. This is very embarrassing. It's incredible to me that he can't see that. How do I make him realize that what he wears counts, even if we're entertaining at home?

First of all, you have to recognize that what he wears doesn't always count. If you can find the distinction between casual times like buddies coming over for a game and your parents sitting down to dinner, then you will be able to find a compromise a little more easily. Chances are that he knows that some of his decisions are ridiculous, but he doesn't want to be your dress-up doll. Look the other way when he wears his twenty-year-old ripped-up sweatpants and sleeveless shirt when his friends are over and he might be more inclined to wear the monkey suit for the more posh company.

A-fuckin'-men. It goes with the advice I gave earlier (unless the editor destroyed my flow): Give men freedom and you'll actually control them more.

Let me be me when it's really not that important. Then I'm all yours. That's what they mean by "choose your battles."

My wife is constantly dieting. She's on and off a new diet all the time. She'll lose some weight, then put it back on and start again. Her diets are ridiculous. They promise quick weight loss, and, for the most part, are different ideas on how to starve your body. I can tell she's on a diet because the starvation aspect of it will go to her brain, and she gets hot-tempered and short with me. It's obnoxious and I can actually see this breaking us up. What can I do to get my wife to just eat right instead of crash dieting?

Well, maybe you shouldn't have been jiggling her fat!

You can start by telling her exactly what you just told us: This might cause the relationship to end. That might be the eye-opener that she needs. Include in this speech that you love her and feel like she's hurting herself, and that you know that there are better ways for her to reach her goal. Offer to be a support for her if she picks better means of approaching her target. Prepare for tears.

Then remember to ignore those tears. They're a defect that needs to be ignored.

When I met my wife, she had long, beautiful hair. About a year ago she cut it short. Though I think that she's still pretty, there's something about long hair on a woman that, to me, is so much sexier than a short do. My wife has continued to cut her hair to keep the short hairstyle. Is there a way for me to ask her to change her look without her assuming that I think she's ugly?

Look, I'd love to wear a diaper all day in my private life. I have a successful business I helped create, I don't really have a boss, and I have most things under control. Why can't I wear a diaper if I want? I think I've earned it. I'll tell you why. Because I live with a lover, and it's all give and take. That's the way I want it, in fact. Sometimes you can't do whatever you feel like.

Don't be scared to tell her your opinion on her hairstyle. Check to see if she even gives a shit.

"I don't like your hair like that so much. I like it long," or "Your hair makes me feel like I'm a homo."

Tell her. She wants to be looked at as hot. She won't mind playing along.

Before the next time she heads over to her appointment at the hair salon, make sure that you comment about how nice her hair already is and that you're surprised that she even feels she needs to change it. Add a little stroking of her locks and remind her how good it feels to have your hands run through her mane. If that doesn't work, next time you have her face down doggie style when you're getting nasty, grab a good chunk of hair and slightly tug on it. Then whisper strongly in her ear about how fantastically nasty it feels to have her held down by her beautiful tresses.

I catch my boyfriend checking out other people sometimes when we're out. I understand that this is part of regular male behavior, but it makes me feel self-conscious that he can't help looking at another woman. Is there anything I can do about this?

It's true that it's normal for a guy to look at women when in public. It's also true that what turns his head is probably turning yours as well. The thing about attractive women is that they attract attention just like anything else shiny, rare, or otherwise eye-catching. Though it's human nature to look at beautiful women, there is also a subtlety to it that your man should have in order to not make you uncomfortable. If he's blatantly staring and being weird about it, maybe you should tell him how you feel. If he insists on continuing, then maybe he's not the one for you.

Yes, you can do something about this. You can grow up.

I've mentioned this in stand-up before, but jokes come from somewhere. Women want a man they can feel safe and secure around—someone they can walk with at night who's aware of his surroundings and has his eye on her safety—but, at the same time, they want a man who's completely oblivious to women sexier than his own. (Sure, we're looking at the fat pigs too—anything different—but that doesn't concern you, does it?) What would you rather have: a guy who notices things around him, including short-skirted hoochies, or a dopey-dumb with his head up his ass? Yes, your man's there to protect you—as long as the attacker isn't wearing a low-cut blouse. Let's hope you two never run into the Glitter Tit Gang. He'll never see it coming.

My husband joined a gym about a year ago. He's joined gyms in the past but always fell off his routine after a couple of weeks. This time around, however, he's been steadily working out since he joined. He is now in great shape. This is fantastic for him, but it has been making me feel more and more out-of-shape and uncomfortable with the way I look. I thought of working out myself, but I don't have time, and I feel like I'm being left behind because of it. I know it's mostly in my head because my husband tells me he thinks I'm beautiful all the time. How do I get my head straight about this?

There is no such thing as not having time to work out. If you're feeling self-conscious, that's on you to change. Make working out and eating better a higher priority in your life or you will destroy your relationship with your insecurities. Wake up earlier or go to bed later. If you work out for only twenty minutes three times a week you will see results.

First, realize that you're not beautiful all the time. He means the *essence* of you is beautiful all the time. Not your looks. *All* the time? Don't be ridiculous.

Second, when he kept falling off his schedule, blaming that he didn't have time as an excuse, you didn't believe him. Of course he doesn't have time to work out. No one *has* time to work out. You *make* time. Later he learned how to make time, and you can too.

You won't feel comfortable again until you work out or burn down his gym. It's your choice, Hog.

My girlfriend takes about an hour to get ready (compared with my ten minutes). That's fine. She looks great when she's done, but she seems to not know how long it takes her to get done. Her routine always makes us late. She knows when we have to leave to make it to where we need to go on time, but somehow she is never ready at that time. Why is this, and what can I do to change it?

Your girlfriend does not respect time. I know because I was the same way, and I still have a few issues with it here and there. It's very hard to change this about a person. They really have to learn it themselves. Your girlfriend has to see how important time is to people. Most people will not tell her that it is an issue that she's late. Most likely, when you show up to events together, they will just say that's it's completely okay and move on with the evening.

It's on you to make her understand how uncomfortable you are showing up late to events.

If that doesn't work, then give her a fake, earlier time that you have to leave the house.

As a man you're expected to play dumb like you believe you're about to leave the house at any moment, meanwhile you know you can catch up on TV or even a nap as you think about how, once again, you're going to be the late couple, and the two of you can lie about the traffic that no one else seems to have gotten caught up in.

I'd say leave without her, but I wouldn't go to a lot of these things if I wasn't half dragged to them, so that's not usually an option. Women love to do Chemda's idea where they tell someone the wrong time, but I'm convinced that eventually they're going to catch on, and it will only make them later when they get a real time for something.

I think you have to call her mom and tell on her.

I recently noticed that my boyfriend has a couple of hairs coming out of his nose and ears. Though it's not turning me off to him because I love him, I do think it's unattractive, and it would be better if he removed it somehow. I don't want to tell him because I think that would embarrass him. How do I make him aware of it while sparing his feelings?

Take your boyfriend to your waxing lady. (If you don't have one, get one. You might need some work done that *he's* not telling you about either.) Warn your waxer that you are bringing your man, and tell her what his issues are. When you go to the bathroom, she will be happy to point out what hairs he needs to have removed. If he agrees for her to do it, it would take no longer than your bathroom break. If he doesn't, he still got told what needs to happen, and he will most likely go home and figure out how to remove the hair himself.

I needed to be told. A guy friend of mine just blurted out, "You don't trim your nose hairs?" I never thought about it, so there was no reason I ever focused on my nose. Once I was told, however, I was grateful. Ever since then I've kept my nose and ears in check. The only thing that upset me about being told is that I wasn't told sooner.

My boyfriend has a favorite hat that he's had for years. He wears it everywhere we go. I asked him to get rid of it because it looks worn out and has a bad smell to it. He refuses. It's starting to drive me nuts to the point of breaking up. Which one of us is being the unreasonable one?

He's being unreasonable, and you might have to break up with him just so that he doesn't forever consider you his woobie killer. If he doesn't know that a hat needs to be sanitary and not unsightly, he's a child. How would he like it if you never washed your hair? He's being silly. If he can't get that then you can't do anything about it.

I get liking an ugly hat, but if it stinks it needs to be washed. That's a rule for most things: If it stinks, it needs to be washed. I'd say to wash it behind his back, but the fact that he has to wear it *every-*

where is just plain disrespectful. Chemda has her favorite dresses, but she'd stop over-wearing one of them for me if I asked.

If this guy's grandma didn't pass the hat down to her grandson—a hat that gave her a reason to struggle and fight through the Holocaust—and she didn't ask him to never part with it and she didn't say to always keep it between himself and Hashem, then leave him if he picks the hat over you. This dude's a douche nozzle. If, however, his grandma really did use this hat to help free some Jewish victims and escape Nazi evilness, then you're kind of being a bitch.

My wife has terrible morning breath, as we all do. I make sure I keep my breath in mind each day, and I brush my teeth before I start talking to her. Why does she not have the same courtesy?

I think that your wife will be pissed no matter how you approach this. Most people have a negative response when they are embarrassed. Approach her gently so that it doesn't feel critical. Tell her something like you were just heading to brush your teeth because you don't want to offend her with your morning breath. Add that you love what toothpaste smells like from her mouth. If that doesn't help, then tell her that you used to date someone who talked to you with morning breath, and it's part of what made you two break up.

I had a girlfriend once who laughed when I told her she had halitosis, as though that was another witty remark from Keith the Comedian. I also had a girlfriend who dismissed my saying she had to brush her teeth three times a day. "No one needs to brush *that* often." She'd laugh it off like I was Robin Williams.

If, however, someone even hinted that I had bad breath, I'd fix it immediately—whatever it took. Some people, however, won't take the hint. In fact, apparently a lot of people won't take a flat-out tell. Yes, try telling her first. She should thank you for the news. However, if she doesn't bite, then you need to treat her like the baby that she is.

When you wake up in the morning, brush your teeth in the sink. Then take the toothbrush, toothpaste, a glass of water, and a large bowl to her in the bed. Without a mocking voice—as though she just came back from surgery and needs this much attention—let her know that you have everything for her to brush her teeth. She'll most likely be so humiliated it came to this that she'll do her duty in the bathroom like a grown adult.

If she does start yelling at you like somehow this is *your* fault, wave your hand in front of your face and cringe: "I'm sorry, I just can't." Then leave the room.

Brains & Personality
(Inner Beauty)

 We know looks are important. It's obviously the first thing you see when you meet somebody and it's what will keep you interested in that person day to day. But don't think I'm shallow. I need the full package. I need beauty on the inside as well. It's just as important as the out.

I used to think you had to settle if you wanted to be with a chick. I used to think that maybe that's why they called it "settling down." I believed you had to pick between the great body and the great personality, and I wondered what I would decide, as they are both very important. Then one day I met Chemda, and I saw what I liked. I loved her body and her singing talent, and I knew I wanted some of that sweetness. I definitely figured she'd have an annoying personality, because I already saw two things I loved, and God only grants so many gifts. After we hit it off the first night we hung out, I was blown away. It seems that God dropped very few surprises on Earth for those willing not to settle. When you have something that's 80 percent the full package to you, and your friends are calling you an idiot for even debating about finding something better, you still have to drop it and continue the search.

It's all important, and it's somewhere out there for those willing to wait. I didn't believe it till I found my 100 percent. I'm not trying to sap it up, I just never had somebody let *me* know that this was possible.

And I'm bragging.

Wow! The way Keith describes me, I should be modeling. That's the thing about attraction: You don't have to be a supermodel for someone to think you're incredible. I highly believe that there is an inside energy that people exude that can make you more or less attractive to someone's eye. This, absolutely, does not mean that you can eat all the pie you want, put on some sweatpants, go to the club with a positively energetic smile and expect people to be excited about seeing you naked; but, if you can maintain a balance of salad, Twinkies, and nice attitude, you might find yourself surrounded by some people who love you.

BRAINS & PERSONALITY (INNER BEAUTY) Questions

I keep hitting it off with girls at the bar. I give them my number and no one calls me back. Why is that?

I hear you. I've had the same problem. These bitches are just scatterbrained, and they keep misplacing our numbers.

For women in bars, the lazy way of saying that they are not interested is to go along with everything you're putting out there, even down to accepting your phone number. It's cruel, and I imagine exhausting for men. There's nothing that you can do to make someone respond honestly when they don't even know you. Don't give up hope. Try talking to girls in a different atmosphere. Women tend to be on guard in bars. Check out other activities happening in your neighborhood and give socializing a try in those places.

My boyfriend burps out loud no matter what company we're in. What's his problem?

He thinks he's being funny. You need to tell him that he's not. His burps do not amuse you or the high-class company you keep. He needs to save it for the bar and his asshole buddies. You need to share some of your own comic stylings with him now. Burp after a nice meal, throw out some pussy farts in bed, and then remind him that perhaps there really is a time and a place for things. Men don't usually find it funny when women scratch their crotch like guys do. Make him choke on his own medicine. In fart form. He'll behave.

Buuuurrrrp!

Good point, baby.

My wife interrupts me constantly while we're out with friends and colleagues. It's very embarrassing. How do I make it stop?

If you haven't told your wife that she cuts you off, believe it or not, she may not know that she's doing it. Next time you're out take mental notes about the disruptions. Make sure that you have some examples. Then, when you're alone again after the gathering, bring this up with her. The very important thing is to not throw the scenarios in her face. Tell her that you want to bring up something that has been on your mind and is very important to you. Explain how it makes you feel when you're being cut off. If she doesn't think that she does it, then remind her with the specific examples that you remembered from that night. A good idea for the next party is to have a signal that you can give her when you feel like she's stepping on your turn to speak. If the sign is subtle enough, then feelings won't get hurt and your point will get across.

It's disrespectful, and it needs to end. Your wife thinks she knows everything, and she's calling you a dummy. Next time she cuts you off, cut her off right back by asking her to pass you some nuts or something over from the next table. You'll get the "eyes" but you'll also get your point across much quicker.

My husband thinks he's funny, but really he just ends up offending friends and family. How can I let him know that his humor falls short?

It's hard to tell someone they're not funny. Everyone is funny to *somebody*. I say you sign him up to open-mic night at the local comedy club. Maybe he's in the right and your family is just a bunch of prude cunts.

Your husband doesn't know that he's being offensive. The people you spend time with are not making it clear, and it seems you aren't either. If you think that opening your eyes wider at him or pinching him is sending the message, you're wrong. What you need to do is remember the topics and situations that you thought were inappropriate, and bring up the details of them to him later that night or the next time you are alone. Let him know specifically why his comments would make people feel odd or uncomfortable. You might be surprised that what was obvious to you was not even a passing thought in his head.

I'm a forty-five-year-old male. I haven't found the right woman yet. Am I being too picky? Should I settle for Miss Almost Right?

It's too easy to question ourselves when things are not going as planned. If your goal was to partner up by a certain age and it hasn't happened, then you may be finding yourself feeling disappointed and very lonely. However, to settle for something as big as a life partner is huge.

Sometimes the goal of a life mate is looked at in a very narrow and short-term way. For example, people think of the wedding, fun reception, honeymoon, et cetera. But that is the most temporary part of the deal. You are signing an agreement to live and be with someone *forever*. Keeping that in mind, what other lifetime contract would you ever sign into, knowing that you're not completely satisfied? Do you want an "almost" perfect life?

Every time you think about settling with a lesser version of what you really want, go to one of your married friends' houses and spend the day with him. The biggest marriage deterrent is marriage.

My girlfriend tries to keep acting like "one of the guys." Why can't she be prim and proper like the other ladies?

Your girlfriend is not prim and proper. That is why she behaves not prim and proper. What was she like when you first met her? I bet she wasn't in a sundress talking plans of her next tea party. You probably liked how aggressive and comfortable she was because she's "not like the other girls." It's probably you who changed your mind about how you feel about being with someone like her. So, what do we do now?

Personally, I'm on your side. Most men want their women to act like women. They're not asking them to walk around with a parasol; they just like their guy buddies to be the jackasses, not their woman. Is that sexist? Maybe, but that's just the way it is. It's funny when

Joey puts a car battery to his testicles. It's not funny when Mary does the same thing to her vagina lips. Maybe it's interesting as a YouTube video, but not funny when it's your lady.

But still, while I am on your side, Chemda's right as rain. She was this "free spirited" when you met her. That can't be changed. Accept it or move on.

When my boyfriend gets drunk, he gets aggressive and starts picking fights with people. He usually uses the excuse that they are looking at me funny or disrespecting me. I feel like he thinks he's protecting me in some way, but really he's just making me feel uncomfortable. I would really like this to stop. What do I do about it?

Your boyfriend is insecure. What can you do about this? Tell him how uncomfortable you are about being fake protected. Tell him that it makes you feel on guard and unsafe. Add that because of his constant bad behavior due to misreading almost every situation, you don't trust him to protect you when there is a reason for response.

Your boyfriend's a douche. He's the one in the bar starting fights that he knows will never go anywhere. He's fake, and he's a pussy.

Hire somebody to lock eyes on your boyfriend when he's drunk. This will set your loser lover off; your man will ask, "What the fuck are you looking at?" and the man you paid will show him by punching him square in the face.

Your man needs to be taken down a peg.

I also recommend that you pay the man you hired in advance,

because it might be awkward exchanging money in front of your boyfriend.

My wife is so shy that when we are out in public, people think she's snubbing them because of how quiet she tends to be. I know that she's a good person, but I think she sends out the wrong signal. I would love for her to come out of her shell. What can I do to help her be more social when we're out?

I used to be shy. It's quite crippling. It's a constant struggle to try to fit yourself into a situation that you feel completely inadequate about. Most of the time you end up just leaving yourself out of any interaction despite desperately wanting to join in. The wrong thing to do to your wife is to call her out in public and force her into conversations in social situations. It'll just end up shutting her down even more. Shy people need to learn about their shyness. I am not kidding when I say that you and she should read up about how to deal with being shy. There are books and websites about how other people coped and overcame. I know that I'm making it seem like it's a deadly disease, but believe me: It'll work much better than "Come on, snap out of it."

Give her five to ten sentences to use in regular conversations, have her practice her smile, and take this robot to a party with you. People really only say the same dumb shit in general anyway, and they're only "conversing" to hear themselves talk. Have her go conversation by conversation using simple sentences like "Wow, how do you do it?" and "Thank you, that's very nice of you to say." A classic is "I'm not sure about that subject, so I'm really not sure how to respond." She'll get along famously, and soon she won't be overwhelmed by people. The next thing you know, she'll have the confidence to voice her own human thoughts.

Being with my wife has always been some of the most loving and fun moments of my life. However, when we are in public, she tends to get very flirty with other men. Sometimes I can pass it off as being playful, but other times it can make me feel so uncomfortable that I want to hide or just leave the party altogether. I have even seen it make other people feel funny. I don't want her to think that I am a jealous person, but I am getting painfully anxious at even the thought of going out with her knowing that there is a huge potential for this to happen. How can I change this?

Your wife needs attention that goes beyond what you are capable of giving her. This is not your fault. You could be swooning over her day and night and she would still need the comfort of other men's attention. The instinctive response is to give her a taste of her own medicine—to be even more flirty and inappropriate just to get a response. Only negative results can come of this. Either she will become angry with you (and then both of you will be mad) or it will just give her permission to indulge in her bad behavior. What you have to do is tell her why you think what she's doing is out of line and that if she continues to do it you will fuck her friend.

People like attention, and by giving attention through flirting, your whore wife gets attention back. She doesn't see people rolling their eyes; she only sees people smiling back at her.

Everyone wants to feel wanted, but she's going a little overboard.

I say fuck her friend.

My wife drives me nuts when she talks to people about subjects that she cares about a little too much. She has these topics of conversation that she can't possibly believe that everyone wouldn't be interested in. I feel like my job at parties is to "save" all the people who are nodding their heads at her lengthy one-sided banter. It's exhausting, and it needs to stop, but I don't know how to tell her. Please help.

 When Chemda says something at a dinner party that I find boring, I make the yawn sign with my mouth and hand. "Snooze Alert in three . . . two . . ." Then I lay my head down on the table. "Go ahead, honey." Everyone enjoys it. It's a real hoot.

 It is not on you to save other people from your wife's conversation. That being said, if you feel you must be responsible for her actions, here is a fantastic way to convey the message: Find a way to subtly videotape her at the next party you go to. In fact, videotape the conversations from the back of her head. From this angle, when she watches the tape, she will only see the person's reaction to her dumb stories. Pass her some popcorn and watch as lessons are learned.

My wife is a know-it-all. She never says she doesn't know something. She has given people tons of wrong information just so she doesn't have to admit that she has no clue about the

subject. It's ridiculous and a huge turnoff to me. She cuts people off midsentence, volunteers facts that aren't true, and corrects people without knowing a thing about the topic. How do I get her to stop talking and just listen?

I despise these people. You can't learn anything at a party because she's always there spouting her bullshit while talking over a real answer. She even, deep down, knows she doesn't know what she's talking about. She just has to be seen as the smartest at the table. She knows it all, except she doesn't know everyone can see through her bullshit, and they're sick of it too. Well, does she know that the taste of a little oven cleaner in her coffee every day isn't noticeable to the human senses? I'm not saying poison your wife, I'm saying— Oh, wait, I just reread what I wrote. I am saying to poison your wife.

Your wife is a bitch, and you are a pussy. I'm sure she's been responding like this for quite some time, and I bet you just sit there and pretend like her words are God-sent. What's wrong with you? Speak up. If you can't fix her chatter when it's happening, set her straight later. Next time you come home from a party, look up the information she passed as truth and give her the real facts. Inform her that she's not fooling anyone. If you don't tell her, who will?

My wife is so nosy. It's just getting worse. She will try to find information relentlessly. She's so shameless. I recently caught her asking our close friends some very inappropriate questions. Then of course she shares this information with everyone. How can I get my wife to mind her own business?

Here's the plan: You set up a story that's bullshit. For example, your cousin is pregnant. The thing is, it's a secret, and she can't tell anyone, including the cousin. She'll go crazy trying to hold it in. Then throw another secret at her: Your best buddy got a sex change and is now dating someone who has no idea. But she can't tell anyone. Not your buddy, not his date. Her head will literally explode. Take her to the hospital, get her head taped up, and then point out how dangerous gossip is.

Or . . . tell her that your friend was asking about abortions the other day, so you mentioned to him that your wife has had two already. Tell her that your buddy was very interested to know that the first abortion went smoothly, whereas her genital wart outbreak got in the way of her second, so there were minor complications. Express that it was really good to have all of this information, and that you never knew that it would come in so handy. Give her at least five minutes of freak-out time, and then let her in on the lesson.

When my husband and I have company over our place he thinks it's appropriate to turn on the TV. I think this stumps conversation and defeats the purpose of having people over in the first place. How can I get him to see that TV ruins our time with friends?

You can't be in complete control of how you want your husband to socialize. While you think that the TV stumps conversation, he might think it gets the conversation started. Why not decide what kind of night it's going to be before the guests come over? You can both decide based on the social setting of the company you will be keeping. Compromising will set your mind at ease rather than having you feel constant anger all night in anticipation of when the remote reaches his hands.

When you and your friends get together, perform little skits for your man based on his favorite TV shows. Act out exciting dramas and hilarious sitcoms. Nothing's better than live theatre. We all can admit that. Now he gets his "TV," and you get your friends interacting with each other.

Preferably, make friends with people the likes of George Clooney or Kiefer Sutherland.

My wife says yes to everything. "Yes, I'll work the bake sale," "Yes, I'll pick up your kids," "Yes, I'll drive you to the airport." Sometimes she's not even being asked a question and she'll respond with a "yes." She's just as busy as everyone else is, and it's not fair to her even if she brings it on herself. How do I get her to stop?

Your wife is sweet and well intentioned and I'm sure she suffers a lot from her illness. She's trying to please everyone and ends up losing herself for other people. Ultimately, she pains herself for no reason and resents the position she puts herself in. To change this aspect of her personality will take time. You can start by telling her that every time she says yes to other people, she's saying no to herself and her own family. That realization alone can be huge. The next part of the process will be you reassuring her every time she says no to someone that she is not a horrible person. After a while she will have an easier time deciding what projects to take on, which to pass on, and saying no will feel empowering.

Chemda has this disease. She goes above and beyond for friends and even acquaintances. I even have to remind myself that I'm not being an asshole by not taking up some of these things she unnecessarily volunteers for.

She's gotten a lot better. She's just a very nice person, and she needed to be taught and reminded that you don't have to be everything to everybody. Sometimes—many times—it's okay to let someone else figure out their own life so that you can enjoy yours.

My girlfriend misuses words constantly. Words like _ironic_ and _ignorant_ get abused in public. Every time this happens, I feel stupid myself. I feel like she's representing me, but I know the meanings of those words. I feel like we need to sit down for a vocabulary lesson. Is this a bad idea?

It sounds like your girlfriend is misusing some of the most commonly misused words. That doesn't make it right, but it does make her look less stupid. Sit with her and talk about it. Don't make this meeting so dramatic that she thinks you're about to tell her she has AIDS, and don't get that holier-than-thou tone that you get. (You know how you do.) Just tell her that you noticed her use of words were a little off a couple of times. If she doesn't agree with you about the words' meanings or doesn't like that you brought up the matter, you can decide how much that weighs on your relationship and go from there. If you never bring it up, you will always be annoyed.

Oh, you're one of those. Listen, Word Snob, no one's noticing her mistakes like you think they are, and, even if they did, they literally wouldn't care.

Yes, *literally*.

You're a hard-on, and you're not fun when you try to correct everyone's shit. Everything's a pet peeve to you. You know what else? You're not as bright as you think. You misspeak constantly, but no one says anything about it because you're not fun to argue with. You're girlfriend's talking good. Don't worry about it.

My wife loses her temper in traffic. If someone cuts her off, for example, she loses it. She will race traffic to get to the offending vehicle to flip off the driver. She's normally really sweet, but she seems crazy to me when this happens. I feel like it's dangerous, and I want it to end. Can I make her stop somehow?

You know those fake cops people hire for bachelor and bachelorette parties? "You're under arrest. I'm kidding. I'm just trying to make some money to go to college. I'm gonna get naked now." You hire one of those to cut off your wife in traffic. She'll then chase the vehicle down, shout her obscenities, threaten to start a fight, and that's when the stripper will get out of his car and reveal that he's an officer of the law. Not the Sex Law, but the regular law. And no boom box of any kind. He'll get out of the car with the cop clothes on, give her the riot act (without a sexy wink), and then he'll go back into his car with his clothes still on.

This might be my best advice yet. There is no way this can go wrong.

I love going nuts in traffic. The adrenaline rush is great, and the whole thing feels awesomely bad-ass. I had to stop most of that behavior because people started telling me how scared they were being in the car with me. I thought they were kidding at first. Who doesn't like a good car race on the highway at a hundred miles an hour? When I saw how serious they were, however, I stopped. (Mostly.)

Tell your wife how intense this behavior is to you. Tell her how you worry about her license being taken away, your insurance being affected, and, most important, your concern about a bad accident.

My husband tends to fake laugh when he's uncomfortable. I find him giggling in conversations with people when there's no joke. I wish he would feel more relaxed socializing. Can I help him get better?

I used to be like that. Not out of insecurities I had, but as a favor so that other people felt more comfortable—like they're the King of Comedy. I stopped when I had a corny roommate that made fake laughing unbearable to me. He'd make bad jokes all the time, and it was exhausting to humor him. After that, I stopped trying to appease everybody. Now people see that when I laugh it's for a reason, and they feel even prouder of themselves. Let your man know that people would like to earn his laugh. They don't want freebies. Tell him to relax. They're doing the talking, and *he's* uncomfortable? That'd be like going to a comedy club where the stand-up act is cool as a cucumber but the audience is sweating. It doesn't make sense.

Your husband thinks he's doing the right thing. He thinks he's helping everyone he talks to. It's actually coming from a sweet place. I assume you know that, and that fact doesn't help you feel better about it.

Your husband is causing every conversation to be way more difficult than it needs to be. He's not letting people gauge their own chatting skills with him. Usually I can tell when someone is just humoring me with their responses. It makes me not want to talk to them. I would much rather get an honest response than a laugh every minute.

Next time you're out, try to remember a conversation between your husband and someone else. Bring it up on the ride home. Say something like "Wasn't Bob so boring? He always thinks he's funny." When your husband agrees with this statement, ask him why he was laughing so much. That will start the conversation gently. Then tell him that you read in a book that fake laughing actually makes other people feel less funny and more uncomfortable. (This is the book, by the way.) The people making the bad jokes keep the one-sided conversation going for the same reason the fake laugher does: Both parties are just being polite.

If your husband uncomfortably chuckles at *this*, just crash the car.

My wife is a lawyer. She is so excited by her career that she talks about it all the time when we're with company. I am happy for her, so I want to hear about the happenings of her day, but I feel like she bores people when she explains the inner workings of the law. How do I get her to know that no one else cares?

I actually know a lawyer who loves to talk about the law all the time, even when what he's saying doesn't apply to anything anyone else brought up. These people need to understand that maybe in the social ladder of jobs they're up there, but in the end, no one really gives a shit. In fact, this just in: Most people hate lawyers. A lot of us think they're ruining this country. Besides, I'll Google the new proposition banning gay marriage on the computer if I'm interested. The lawyer's not gay, I'm not gay, and no one in the room is gay. We all give no fucks.

I think to make these people understand this you have to be blunt. I use humor and false self-deprecation to take the sting out of my blunt comments.

"I don't follow this stuff. I'm dumb."

They'll try to help you. "No, don't say that. It's simple. The government imposes a seven-ten levy on all overtures regulated locally—like in New York, for example—and then the interest of that compounded upon itself—"

"Yeah, I don't care. I don't know this stuff. I'm dumb. Let's get back to Angelina Jolie's babies."

You flat-out said you don't care, but you somehow made it seem like it's your fault. Now, the lawyer no longer shares his stories with me, and I'm home free. Plus, *I* know I'm not dumb, so who cares? How am I sure I'm not dumb? I just tricked a lawyer!

Take this type of idea and use it on your wife. Explain to her that everyone's not as smart as she is, and, because of that, they could give a shit about her day-to-day work. Luckily you like to hear her stories, and that works out nice. Have her save her work-related stories for the nights you stay in with a glass of wine (that no one but you two can appreciate) and a box of Trivial Pursuit question cards.

I'm with Keith. I'm dumb, too. Please don't bother.

I noticed that my girlfriend kisses people hello on the lips. I don't think it means anything because it seems to be a casual thing for her to do, but I'm still a bit uncomfortable with it. Am I being a prude or do I have a case here?

I know some people who kiss on the mouth as a simple hello. I never understood it. I think it's an invasion of personal space and is way more intimate than, for example, a handshake or a kiss on the cheek. I always feel uncomfortable when people do it to me, and I feel uncomfortable seeing it done to Keith.

I don't usually say anything about it because I know that the same friends of mine who are kissing Keith on the mouth when they just met him a week before are the people who kiss their cousins, siblings, and parents on the kisser. I know it doesn't mean anything sexual, so I just chalk it up to it being a tradition that I am not accustomed to. You have to decide if you can shrug it off or not.

I love it. What a beautiful way to say hello to a pretty woman. This world can always use more demonstrations of love. My only problem is remembering who is a kisser and who isn't. Nothing is more awkward than when a girl is about to platonically kiss your mouth hello, but you go for the cheek. The mouth redo never works.

"I forgot you're a mouth kisser. Let's do that again."

No dice. Too late.

That's why I started putting a star next to the contacts in my phone who are mouth kissers. I didn't want to ever miss out again.

That said, I decided to stop receiving the kisses because Chemda didn't like it. She says she "shrugs it off," but if it's a thing for her, then why do it? I just have to wait till her heart softens up, I guess.

So it's up to you. Keeping in mind that you can kiss ladies on the mouth now, are you still opposed to it? I wasn't. I loved it. If you are okay with it, enjoy. I don't know how it's okay, but enjoy.

The Internet

 When Keith and I first met, he was running and maintaining his website SHITE.com. At the time the site contained an early draft of his autobiography that people could download for free. He would also update it often with short stories about his daily existence. He happened to mention the site when we first got a real chance to speak, but, in all honesty, I would have found it on my own as soon as I got home. Some people say it's a stalker move to Google someone. I say it's dumb not to. There are so many people blogging and twittering and leaving information out for the public to see. They have to keep in mind that some part of the public will be the people they are trying to sleep with.

I learned a lot about Keith through his site. I read all about his childhood and current lifestyle. Instead of asking him things like "What are you looking for in a girl?," I was able to ask about more personal matters, such as: "How didn't you learn about masturbation until you were eighteen?"

There are, of course, downsides to the Information Super-highway. For example, the guy who you've been chatting with on-line who you thought was so clever, quick, and witty meets you for coffee, and it turns out typing is the only comfortable way he has to interact with humans. You both just sit there staring at each other until your coffee gets cool enough to throw down your throat, and then you escape. Or maybe you two are really hitting it off online, and during a chat session you type something sarcastically but you forget to put the tongue-face emoticon to show how "just kidding" you were, and then a fight breaks out over a bad "yo mama" joke.

The Internet is a great tool, but it can be tricky. You have to keep in mind how your online interactions agree with your non-Internet persona.

Is it normal to instant-message each other when you are sitting in the same room?

Is it cheating if an avatar is blowing your boyfriend while it's chat-moaning, "Mmmm . . . you taste so good"?

Are you okay with your boyfriend posting his penis on the Net if he discreetly calls himself 2hot4u6969?

These silly things need to be answered now so that they don't turn into big things later. I will answer my sample questions for Keith so there are no misunderstandings.

Yes, it is normal.

Enjoy your virtual "blow job" and try not to think about the fact that this is most likely a man typing back on the other end who's slowly applying lipstick as he brings you to climax.

If 2hot4u69 is already taken, don't add an extra "69" and think you're clever. The least you can do is come up with a good fake name.

THE INTERNET Questions

I've been dating a guy for three months now and he still has his ex-girlfriend as his number one friend on MySpace. Should I be concerned?

You should be as concerned as he is about it. People get *obsessed* with social networking sites like MySpace. They post new information about themselves daily, link pictures as soon as they get them, and give friends constant updates about their feelings. How into the whole MySpace thing is your boyfriend, generally speaking? If your new boyfriend is still very involved with it, then yes, his ex's friend status might mean something. If he hasn't made an update in months, then no worries.

Assuming that you two are very close after these three months, I say that if he updates and follows his MySpace regularly, then yes, there's cause for concern. He checks his messages and mail, and also notices who's on his Friends List. He especially notices who's #1, and by keeping his ex up there, he's probably sending a message to her. If he pretends not to understand what the big deal is, then you can counter by saying, "What's the big deal of removing her altogether?"

I usually wouldn't get caught up in Internet networking site silliness, but this one could potentially mean something.

I've been lonely for a while and thought of signing up to an Internet dating site. Does that make me look desperate?

It depends on what you write in your profile. Don't worry about looking desperate. Some of the most popular sites on the Internet are dating sites. People are meeting through the Web all the time. It's just another way to reach someone you might like. If it makes you feel odd to post on an official dating site, start slower. Join a forum or a chat group on the Net that talks about something that interests you. For example, if there is a TV show or hobby that you're into, find a site that focuses on it. The conversation will be easier because you'll be talking about something you have in common. Chances are that the people you're chatting with have in-person meet-ups that you can be a part of. It's a lot less pressure than meeting on a first date, and it will show you what it feels like to meet a person digitally before physically.

Of course you're not desperate. The Internet is the hottest new club, and the stigma of meeting people online has gone away. In fact, more couples I know my age met online than in person. When they instant-message each other a virtual martini, that's a little strange, but all other interaction is normal.

If anything, a dance club is weirder to get to know somebody in. Everyone's drunk, on guard, trying to cop a feel before last call. My only advice is that when you fill out your online profile, don't write "Sucking and Fucking" under hobbies. I didn't get one single e-mail response. (True story.)

I'm married to a great woman and have been very satisfied by her, but I have recently been entering sexual chat rooms and participating in anonymous dirty talk. Does that count as cheating?

It sounds like the answer is yes because you're asking. It sounds like you're doing this when your wife is not around, and that she would highly disapprove. If you wouldn't be allowed to talk to these people like this over the phone, then you're not allowed to share your poisoned filth with them in a chat room.

Ask your wife anyway. Maybe when you're playing your games, she's in the other room typing with one hand as well. Maybe you're chatting with each other. "If you like piña coladas . . ."

It's seems so innocent when it's you doing the chatting, but imagine if you walked by your wife while she was on the computer and she suddenly minimized or closed the window she was working with. The deception is the problem here. This topic is similar to husbands wanting to go to strip clubs. Some wives are okay with it, but if the women who don't approve of it catch their men coming home with glitter on their crotch and smelling like peachy-whore perfume, you're going to have issues.

My boyfriend spends a lot of time on the Internet. He even has people whom he calls his "Internet friends." Is this normal? Can I lose him to a computer?

We made our bones with the Internet, so yes, it's very normal to have special online friends. And encouraged.

Seriously, I have Internet buddies. I've met a lot of them in real life, but I knew them first online. Others I still haven't met, but enjoy chatting with them.

As long as the Internet isn't taking time away from the two of you being together, there's nothing strange about it. That's assuming that all his friends aren't at LatexFucking.org.

Getting caught up in anything too much is not healthy. He can lose himself to the Internet. Internet friends are okay, but not if you spend all your time online with them. The Web can feel very safe and friendly. It can make you feel like you're with a bunch of friends when you're really at home by yourself. This is great for a little while, but the Internet has its own way of interacting that is not the same as in-person conversations. Since socializing in public is a habit you have to practice, too much Internet communication can throw someone's social skills off.

Tell your boyfriend that you want to hang out with him and come up with fun events and outings. If that and the offer of sex doesn't work, he's a goner.

I have a long-distance relationship with my boyfriend, and the Internet helps us stay connected. Recently, he has asked to have chat sex. I would love to participate, but have to say that I have no idea how to do that or where to even begin. I want to fulfill his fantasies. Please help me!

As with getting kinky in person, you should remember that *he* thinks he's the nervous one. He thinks you have it under control. But someone needs to initiate. Just throw out some simple sex talk, and watch how well he catches on. It was his idea after all. He won't leave you hanging. Virtually play with his dick: uu===D; then tell him how much his body doesn't suX0rs, and finish off by letting him know how you'd love him to come inside you FTW!!!!!11111!1!1 He'll be pwned in no time.

Start practicing typing with one hand.

If you're chatting with no camera, then you just have to type what you would normally want to tell him if you were on the phone. Things like how you miss him and wish he was inside you. Tell him what you think of when you masturbate. (Leave out any fantasies that do not include him or his awesome ways.)

If you have a camera, that takes it to the next level. Most camera programs come with verbal chat options. You both will be able to do anything you want but physically touch. You can wear lingerie and show him what he's missing when he's away. Don't forget to turn off the camera so that your domestic affair remains unnoticed.

A girl I've been chatting with, but haven't met yet, sent me a picture of herself naked over the Internet. She's smoking hot, and she seems nice, but is that a red flag/warning sign that she's crazy?

Take a chance and find out the fun way. Fuck her and see what happens.

It's a warning sign that she's fun, sexual, and not here to play games. If that's what you want, go for it. Does this mean she's probably damaged in the ways that all fun girls are? Absolutely.

My girlfriend and I chat on the Internet a lot when we're not around each other. We both have webcams, but she hardly ever wants to turn her camera on. Should I be suspicious?

Your woman might be more insecure than you are aware of. She might not be turning her camera on because she doesn't have her makeup on, didn't do her hair, the lighting is bad, et cetera. I hate having a webcam on me because it can make me feel self-conscious. It's fun sometimes, but to have it on all the time can feel like you're being watched stalker-style. Besides, the camera is directed at one place. She can have the camera on all the time with another man there and you would never know. Does that make you feel better?

If she was cheating, she'd probably put the camera on just to show you *nothing* is going on. We got Columbo over here, peeking at the edges of a webcam looking for clues in the mirrors. Relax. Like Chemda said: If she is cheating on you, you won't know by her camera anyway.

But yes, she's cheating on you. These feelings don't come from nowhere.

I'm twenty-five and have been thinking of my high school sweetheart. Would it be super creepy to look him up on the Internet?

With social sites like Facebook and MySpace, people like to be found. To find these people and try to start a relationship like you had before is creepy. I'm not saying I haven't tried shady things like that. I used 9/11 as an excuse to call up exes.

"Just wanted to see if you're okay. I was thinking about you."

"I live in Nevada, Keith. I'm fine."

"Just wanted to make sure. So . . . what are you wearing?"

But if you can resist telling him how you'd like a final bang, I think it's fine to dial up an ex. Look them up at least. Are they married with kids? Maybe they got a sex change. I know my high school girlfriend Shannon lives near where she was born and didn't accomplish any of her life goals. HOW'S THAT JOURNALISM DEGREE WORKING OUT NOW? MAYBE YOU SHOULDA STUDIED MORE INSTEAD OF MAKIN' OUT WITH OTHER DUDES! *WE WERE GONNA GET MARRIED!!*

Keith is right. Don't lead with how much you've been thinking about him and how you think you can build a life together. First of all, you are thinking about a guy you knew just after his balls dropped. People change a lot ten years after high school. Make sure that he is what you remember him to be before you get all happy about dating your fifteen-year-old boyfriend again. Second, if he didn't want to be found, he wouldn't be on the find-me sites that Keith mentioned.

My wife recently got very involved with the Internet. She suddenly finds it important to post things like our pictures and daily activities. I find some of this to be distasteful, and I feel like sharing our personal information with the world is very odd. What is this need that she has, and can I make it stop?

It's exciting to share stories, and sharing information is now easier than ever. She doesn't understand how strange this is to you, and you'll want to redefine what is for the public and what things are only for the two of you.

Posting information on the Internet can make people feel like their lives are more special than they really are. The fact that people can see and follow a person's life can make them feel like a celebrity. On the other hand, people often post their information to allow relatives and close friends to be updated on their goings-on. Either way, it doesn't mean that she can take liberties with your privacy and do with it as she pleases. Set boundaries just as you would any other thing that makes you feel uncomfortable. You have the right to decide what of your life is public and what remains private.

My boyfriend is part of a community that meets on the Internet to play games together. He plays online with people all over the world. I was never able to really get into it, but he seems like he has a lot of fun when he's playing. Nothing ever bothered me about this activity until just recently. He told me that the players in our area are planning a live get-together that he wants to go to. He will be meeting people whom he otherwise only communicated with online. This seems dangerous and scary to me. What should I do?

You should trust that he knows what he's doing. Any situation *can* turn into a dangerous one, but chances are that he is familiar enough with whom he will be meeting based on the time he spends with them online. Gamers usually talk while they play, whether it be via typing or headphones and microphone. Chances are that he knows some of his online buddies better than most of the people he works with.

There's nothing to be afraid of. These people are shy and introverted for the most part. The most dangerous thing you'll encounter is being bored to death by a story on how the new game interface is totally a step back from the original one.

I recently started dating a great woman. After introducing her to a pal of mine, he mentioned that she looked familiar to him. A couple days later he remembered why and sent me an e-mail with an attached photo of my new woman topless. He saw it because she was featured in one of those Girls Gone Wild–type sites. I was very embarrassed. I asked him to not mention this to anyone else we know, but I just feel like if he found it, other people I know can also. Is this worth dumping someone over?

Seems like no one can get away with doing anything without it being posted somewhere on the Internet. This picture could be the result of a single night of drunken fun, and she's probably unaware that it has been posted for everyone to see. The photo can be removed by simply sending an e-mail to the website owner and Internet service provider.

On the other hand, if you do a search for her name and find that it is synonymous with Can't-Keep-Her-Clothes-On-McGee, then this probably won't be the last fun e-mail with attachments that you get from your friends.

Didn't you always want to be with a fun girl like this?

If you don't want a girl who thinks it's fun having her picture online, then you don't want this girl. It sounds like she didn't take this picture that long ago. This is who she is. Don't dump her because you care what your friends think; that's lame. But if this is unacceptable to you personally, you have to do what you have to do.

My husband and I spend a lot of time apart during the week. Work, the kids, and running errands keep us so busy that most of the day we have to communicate via our cell phones. I would love to be able to have more face-to-face time with him, but I understand the circumstances and the importance of needing to prioritize. My problem with this, however, is the way he communicates. Instead of calling me, he'll send me text messages all day long. I understand that at work it's hard or impossible to be on the phone, but once he gets out of his office, why isn't he just calling me?

How many nonconversations would you like to have with your husband all day long? Texting to remind you to pick up milk while you're at the store is a lot more efficient than calling and making with the fake niceties. If it seems cold, then you need to remedy that without forcing inane and unnecessary chat. Instead of asking for a call every time you and he need to communicate something simple, schedule a call each day to talk about your thoughts. This call should have nothing to do with errands or your children. One real call a day will be less strained and more romantic than trying to keep him on the phone when he called about which toilet paper you prefer.

Maybe if you knew what "I really have to get off the phone" meant to begin with, then he wouldn't have to hide in text form. How many times do you need to say good-bye before he knows which one of them counts?

"Watchya doin'?"

What the fuck you think he's doing? He's buying toilet paper!

I have been part of an online community for about a year now. We leave comments for each other on our message boards and chat often on a video chat site. A lot of people in this group are people whom I consider my friends and a very important part of my life. Recently, my wife asked if she can join in this community. Though I love my wife, I really want to keep this "society" to myself. Am I being selfish?

Wanting to keep something to yourself is the definition of selfish. So what? If she joined a knitting circle, would you have to be a part of that?

If the community is Keith and The Girl, then yes, you're being selfish. Everyone should be a part of this community, get the KATG logo tattooed on them, and spread the word like it's the Second Coming of Christ.

If it's not, then it's fine for you to keep this for yourself. Open your own mail, have your own bank account, and keep your own Internet community where you can have your silly fun—unless the community's some weird racist child-fucking freak show. You can't trick me into okaying awful shit.

My wife and I have been exploring videotaping ourselves while we have sex. We've gotten some real excitement from watching them back. We want to now take this idea to the next level and put our videos on the Internet. Is this a bad idea?

You do realize that everybody has access to the Internet now, right? Like everyone. Your boss, your mother, your next-door neighbor . . . everyone. Do you also know that porn is one of the most popular things that people search and use the Internet for? Now, knowing that, do *you* think it's a bad idea?

If people get excited by your video, they will try to look you up. Cross-referencing ClaireHunt007 with your other screen name, ClaireinNYC, isn't that hard. If you don't mind a Google search of your name leading to a video of your wife getting the ol' salami the way Nature didn't intend, then by all means, upload. If not, invest in costumes.

My girlfriend is a very intelligent and mature woman. Why is it, then, that when we type online to each other she sounds like an idiot? She types in that weird Internet child-speak. It drives me nuts and makes me respect her less. I know that everyone is picking up on Internet lingo, but is it wrong of me to not be able to tolerate it coming from the person I'm dating?

Lolz. U r so funz. Yo bitch be playin n u be hatin. No worries dog. Leav dat byatch alone.

Totes.

I am not Internet savvy at all. I mostly use my computer to e-mail, watch videos, and do silly searches. I hear that a lot of people are hooking up through websites and general online activity. I feel like I'm missing out on connections with the opposite sex because I don't know how to use the Internet right. What am I missing?

Internet hookups and live hookups both start with something in common: You have to engage. If you know the Internet enough to do those silly searches of yours, then use that to search for online dating sites, singles chats, and meet-ups. The Internet is not a secret. You just have to admit what you want and type it in. Then delete your autofill and your cookies. No one needs to know why you did a search for guys with girl parts.

Every time you meet someone online, you know that behind their silly Internet name is a real person. Real people like to fuck.
You're caught up now. Go get 'em.

My boyfriend and I have been using the same desktop computer since we moved in with each other four years ago. He is now talking about getting a laptop for himself. Does this mean that he wants to separate us somehow or that he wants to hide things from me?

I get most everything off the Internet: Our talk show began and flourished on the Internet; I get my local, national, and world news online; I hear tunes through my computer speakers . . . He's not necessarily trying to hide things from you. He probably just wants to use the computer when he wants to use it. Rachael Ray's new line of cookware is exciting to look over your shoulder at, but he really wants to see who won the football game back in his hometown. Computers went from being a luxury to practically a necessity, and he finds it'd be easier for everyone if each of you didn't have to wait in line for your turn.

It sounds like you don't trust him at all. If your first response, to what anyone else would consider a practical and fun solution, is that he wants to cheat on you, then your issue is not a new computer. That's kind of like having an issue with him wanting to build you a new bathroom. Do you feel like he loves you less if he doesn't have to wait to brush his teeth because you're dumping? Him getting a new computer means you get your own as well. Rethink what you're mad about.

I've been dating someone for five months now. I like him a lot, but I hate how little he knows about computers. He's one of those people who just gets flustered by new technology and is sort of proud of it. When I ask him to do simple things on the computer, he says things like "You do it. You know I can't understand all these Internet things." This drives me nuts, and though I like everything else about him so far, I am thinking of breaking up with him just because of this. Am I being hasty?

He could be playing dumb, or maybe he really is dumb. Can you handle either?

People love to play dumb to get out of having to do things. I know these people.

"Keith, I don't even know how to copy and paste!"

"Well, you highlight the text you want to copy—"

"Whoa! You can stop right there, 'cause I have no idea!"

It's like when Chemda tries to tell me how simple it is to cook quesadillas.

"After you have your tortilla in the pan, just add your in-gredi—"

"Whoa, baby! I can't understand anything! Looks like this will always be *your* job!"

Or, he's dumb. I don't mean to call my dad out as an example, but parents are the epitome of this.

"Dad, to download the instant messenger you click on the giant DOWNLOAD INSTANT MESSENGER button that takes up half of the screen."

"Whoa! Slow down! Click what?!"

"Click the giant button."

"But under it is a banner where I'm supposed to go virtual fishing, and each 'fish' is an Xbox! I don't want an Xbox!"

"Then don't click the banner. Only click the DOWNLOAD button."

"Whoa whoa whoa! I don't want to be charged for an Xbox! Did I already get charged?!"

So you have to figure out which one of the two your man is. Is he pretending to be dumb, or is he really this dumb? Once you figure out which he is, you have to decide if you can live with that. He won't change. Dummies are dummies, and some people just love not knowing.

Remember that you are not good at *everything*, and you never will be. Have you ever had someone try to explain the mechanics of a car to you when you just want them to fix it? They keep saying things like "It's so easy. Just loop that and mess with this." (I didn't listen either.) You know you can learn a lesson there that would allow you to do it yourself the next time you're having trouble with the car, but you're not interested. That's your boyfriend to you and computers.

There will always be something in the relationship that one person can do that the other struggles with. If you can find a way to accept your role as the IT department in your relationship, then maybe he won't call you stupid when you refuse to learn how the DVR from your cable works.

My wife is connected to her smartphone like crazy. When we're out, she's texting people constantly and checking updates of her favorite website. I feel like I don't have her full attention. She thinks that it's not a big deal and she's not ignoring me because she can multitask. I find this infuriating. How can I make her see that it's not what I want when I'm out with her?

Your wife is being rude. You're right to be upset. Next time you're out, bring a handheld game system with you and play it in the restaurant while you're waiting for your meal. If she thinks you're being ridiculous, tell her that you're with her, and you're listening. Repeat her last sentence verbatim to prove it. (Women hate when you do that.) When she sees how annoying this is, tell her that this is exactly how you feel about the phone.

If she still doesn't get it, start texting her your end of the conversation when you're out. Clearly that's the only way to get her attention.

I used my husband's computer the other night and I noticed that when I was filling in the websites in the browser bar that the autofill suggestions were filthy weird porn sites. I can't imagine my husband watching this kind of thing, as he is a really nice person. Should I ask him about it?

Your husband was curious what you get by typing in these words, so he typed them in. No big deal. That autofill can be a killer. You start Googling "Nazi atrocities," and, the next thing you know, your browser's autofilling in "German Scat Videos." It's unfair. Even if your hubby does likes to see strange things sometimes, that's not abnormal. Let him be.

Amen.

Marriage

 I said it on a DVD, and I only tell the truth when I do stand-up: People ask me often, "If you love your girlfriend so much, why don't you marry her?" I always reply, "For what?" I always get a dumb stare back.

"Is your love so grand that you think it'd be nice to share it with the government? Your way of giving back?"

I get a blank stare in return.

"Was the movie *Blood Diamond* so engaging that you'd like to see a sequel?"

The stare continues.

Many comedians mock the archaic convention of marriage. My lady and I saw comedian Bill Burr onstage. He reminded us how everyone knows that the statistics of a marriage working are well below 50 percent. "If you were going skydiving and they told you half the parachutes weren't gonna open, you'd be like: 'Yo, fuck that; I'm not going!'" Everyone in the club laughed and laughed. The great comic Doug Stanhope asks onstage, "If marriage didn't exist, would you invent it?" We nod to each other how true that is, and how dumb we all are. "Drinks all around."

We laugh. "This guy onstage is funny! And *right!*" Then the audience goes home and everyone dreams about how many white horses will carry *them* to the altar when it's their turn.

"Is this the line to lose half my shit? Awesome . . ."

And you can convince yourself you're doing it for the tax break, but let's be real: It's to fit in. It's to shut up your parents and to show off your ring to your friends. Girls care more about pretty things and attention than men, so that's why girls want to get married more than men. They see all their friends get to dress like medieval princesses, and they need it to be their turn. No one realizes that we don't fight dragons anymore, and you don't have to wear a dress that drags twenty feet behind you.

You laugh. Until it's your turn.

I think another reason people want it to be their turn is because turnabout is fair play. Bridesmaids have to fly to another state, wear an ugly dress and horrendous updo, and then thank the torturer by making a speech about how wonderful they are. Well, guess what, honey? It's my turn. I don't really want these ugly outfits I'm making you wear in my photographs, but you made me do it, so now I'm making you do it. And also, cut your heels an inch shorter. It's *my* day.

You laugh. Until it's your turn.

But you know what? Do it. Get married. Why do I give a fuck? Do I have to live with you? Do we share a room? No. I don't know you. Get married, fuck a goat, and eat a bowl of candy for breakfast. It doesn't affect me. Just remember to let me live my own life. You're not more in love than me because you threw a bouquet at twenty screaming vultures who are begging for it to be *their* turn.

MARRIAGE Questions

My girlfriend and I just got engaged. We're very excited and have begun plans to marry right away. We found out that we have two very different ideas of what a perfect wedding is. I want a small intimate wedding in a remote location, and she wants a huge reception with what seems like anyone she's ever met in her life. How can we possibly compromise on this?

One way to compromise is to meet exactly half-way. Make sure that you have your budget set out, then meet in the middle when it comes to the guest count, the location, and everything else that comes your way. For example, if you want fifty people and she wants two hundred, you compromise at one twenty-five. If she wants it local and you want to get on an airplane, think about somewhere that's just an hour or so drive away. Either that or you can toss a coin. Whoever wins gets to have their kind of wedding now. The loser gets to throw their party in ten years. You'll be together forever anyway, right?

She wants a big wedding. You want a small wedding. Here's how you compromise: You have a big wedding.

Here's the thing: You really don't care. You want it small and hassle-free. She does care. She's cared since she had Barbie's Dream Wedding Adventure Set. And after all the weddings that she got bullied into going to, you're going to take away *her* turn?

Remind her how old-fashioned you are, and that Daddy should pay, and let her have her dumb dream.

I want to ask my girlfriend to marry me. Her friends' wedding rings are nowhere near the kind of jewelry that I can afford. Should I take out a big loan or hope that a smaller ring will do?

It'd be a shame to have to struggle financially to do something so beautiful, but women do care about their ring. Fuck her if she needs something as gaudy as her attention-seeking friends, but the ring does have to be a real diamond. It can't be a cubic zirconia, no matter how down-to-earth she swears she is. If the brides didn't mind a fake engagement ring, they wouldn't pass it off as real. Don't break the bank, but you do have to get something nice.

I always think that a loan is for something real, like a house or a car. To start a marriage with a loan on a piece of jewelry you can't afford seems like an extra strain on a new life together. However, I understand that I am in the minority and that, for the most part, the size of the ring indicates the commitment on the guy's side. I say take out a big loan and make her friends' jaws drop when they see her finger. After you get married, the bills are shared anyway.

I have been thinking about asking my current girlfriend of three years to marry me. My only hesitation is that we're in our mid-thirties and this would be her third marriage if she says yes. Am I wrong to be a bit hesitant about making a commitment to a person who seems to not be able to keep them?

Think of it this way: She *thought* she found true love until she met you. Besides, if it doesn't work out, at least she knows how to fill out the paper-work.

I think about all the silly times I thought I was in love. I told my first real love that we were going to marry each other when we got older, but it fell apart after a wonderful three months. A sweet twelve-week relationship—gone. I was eighteen. When it ended and I met someone else, I thought, "That previous relationship was love? I thought we had something? We weren't even fucking!" YOU HEAR THAT, SHANNON! I'M SOOO OVER YOU! Anyway, my point is: She just made some mistakes like we all have; it doesn't mean that she doesn't take marriage seriously.

Then again, she could be fucking up again. Keep a separate bank account, minimum.

I can't believe that I met the most incredible person in the world. This woman is beautiful, sexy, and smart. Anything I could have possibly thought of that makes a woman perfect for me, she has. I feel like I *have* to marry her or I'm the biggest idiot. My married friends, however, tell me that all of them felt the same way about their spouse, but that things really change after you get married. I can't imagine that my girlfriend could be so different when I feel like I know her so well. Can marriage really change someone so much?

It's not that *things* change after marriage. It's that people change over time and circumstances don't stay the same throughout your life. Think about what mattered to you ten years ago in comparison to what matters now. The tricky part of a relationship, married or not, is that you have to find a way to grow together while remaining true to yourself.

Partnerships tend to change in obvious ways. Maybe you're not picking her up for dates anymore since you live together, so she's not getting all dolled up for you on a regular basis. Or it could be bigger things. Maybe she decided she found Jesus, though you both were practicing Muslims when you met. If you think you will be able to predict everything about your girlfriend and your relationship with her, you will fail. Understand you both will grow, and try not to kill each other over who put the empty milk carton back in the refrigerator.

It's not right that people change. You should be able to go back to the wife you had on Day One. Isn't that why you signed papers? But I guess it doesn't work that way. You have to learn to grow and adapt and blah blah blah . . . After all, if she's changing, chances are you're changing, too.

Maybe she'll be telling you, "But you said you'd never want to do my butt."

And you'll look at her and explain, "Baby, we said a lot of things when we were young. But I've matured. Now turn around."

Fair's fair, and people need to be able to adjust.

I'm twenty-three years old and have been with my high school sweetheart since eleventh grade. I love her very much. She's my best friend, and I want to be with her forever. I told my friends that I'm going to ask her to marry me, and they think I'm crazy. They think that sleeping with just one person your whole life is a mistake and that I should go out and play the field. I never feel like I'm missing something by not having experimented. Am I making a mistake?

When I dated my first boyfriend I couldn't imagine being with anyone else. Everything seemed perfect. I felt understood and loved. I thought I was going to marry him.

Weirdo.

Anyway, I think that feeling is very common. Companionship can feel very comforting and exciting. The first person who makes you feel that way has a huge effect because of it being such a new feeling. The reality is that the haze of that novel feeling makes you forgive too easily, compromise yourself without realizing, and settle without noticing. It also doesn't help that she is probably the first person who touched your pee-pee. Sex is a cloud even adults have trouble clearing. Make sure that she has not been the only person you've interacted with. Make sure you think about what "forever" really means. If you're still up for it, do it. You're an adult, right?

If you two don't have any real issues to deal with in your perfect relationship, then you may not fully know her. In fact, I declare that you do not. You can remedy this with my help.

1) Go camping with her—real camping—for a week. See what crankiness the girl's been hiding. When push comes to shove, can she step up to the plate?
2) Go swimming, pretend you're drowning, and see if she saves you or freaks out.

That's it. If she passes, you're golden.

My husband's best friend is the only remaining single person in our circle of friends. He's always out and looking for the next woman to mess around with. He has never really committed to women on any level in his life. My problem with this is that when my husband goes out with him, I just know that it's a very "single men outing." I feel like his best friend influences him, has him flirt with girls, and generally encourages him to behave like a juvenile. I don't want my husband to lose his best buddy, but how can I make the behavior when they are out more appropriate?

Your husband is a flirter or he's not. He likes to get silly sometimes or he doesn't. His friend isn't the problem. You trust your husband or you don't.

Your husband knows that he's married. He's choosing to stay that way. He comes home to you. He shares his life with you. Don't be so controlling. When he and his single buddy get together, he probably behaves like an ass and lives vicariously through his friend's behaviors. If you don't let him have this time out with his pal, he'll only resent you. If he came to a ladies' brunch with you and sat in on your conversations with your girlfriends about how "cute the UPS man's butt is, tee hee," you might be in trouble, too. Give him the space he needs, and he will continue coming home after his silly beer-drinking, high-five-having, female-judging party.

My boyfriend and I had been together five years when he popped the question. His marriage proposal later came with a request to sign prenuptial papers. He comes from a wealthy family and is a trust-fund baby himself. I make a decent living on my own. Though I would not be considered rich, I have never needed his money to sustain my own life. I am not in this for his riches, so it's odd for me to think that he might think I am. Does a prenup mean that we don't love each other?

A prenup, if only one person has all the money, sounds smart. He's worked hard for his cash. Or his parents did. Somebody did, anyway. Is it a crime that it entered his brain that he needs to protect it? Of course, you're wondering if there's any doubt in his head regarding the relationship. "How can he even *think* we could break up?"

Well, it *could* happen. It just could. You could grow different ways, want different things, or become infertile . . . I've come to the realization that a prenup is okay. You'll be in love forever, so why not sign a prenup just for extra silly peace of mind.

Does a marriage mean you don't love each other? You're signing a contract that says you love each other. Why? Did you not know it already? When you get married, you sign papers promising to love each other forever. You're asking him to contractually love you. He's just adding a clause into your paperwork.

I've been dating someone for five years now. I know that he's the one. I love spending time with him and, as a couple, I think we work very well together. About two years ago, we made the decision to move in with each other. I thought that this move would lead to the bigger commitment of marriage. I've seen nothing that tells me that he is going to make that move anytime soon. I know that marriage is what I want and that just living together will not be enough for me. I think five years of being with each other is enough to know if we want to tie the knot or not. Should I push him to make a decision?

Yes, absolutely push him. You know best.

WAIT! I was being sarcastic! Man, I sure hope you weren't in a hurry and stopped at "Yes, absolutely," because that's going to be a huge mistake.

Too bad you had plans. He didn't. He's not ready. You're going to coerce him to marry you? How wonderful and magical.

You fucked up. Next time don't have secret plans about other people's lives. You can't antagonize someone into enjoying a life with you.

"Should I push him?" My God. I never . . .

Why did you move in with him without talking about what you ultimately want out of the relationship? If you're so adamant about getting married, you should be open about it. You can't just make a commitment in hopes that that will get another commitment to happen. If you're scared to talk to him about this, then you can't get married. Also, you can't *push* anyone to make big life-changing decisions without it having negative results down the line. What you *can* do is tell him your thoughts on moving forward together. Be prepared for your goals not to match. No matter the answer, a real answer from the source is better than reading his mind any day.

I just started dating a guy about two months ago. We were both raised Jewish. I am nonpracticing, but he keeps his diet kosher. I want to know if this has *disaster* written all over it. I don't believe in dating just for fun, and I usually cut things off ahead of time if I see something that will lead to a breakup after things get really serious. He's a great guy, but will our differences in diets be an issue in the long run?

Picture what it means to be with someone who has a different diet from you. In this case, you will have to be the one to compromise. Your house will have to be kosher—food, dishes, and all. Meals out will most likely be held only in kosher restaurants. This extends to when you include your non-kosher friends in your plans. It's on you to decide if this affects how you love a person.

I know many relationships where the woman eats what she wants and the man keeps ~~silly~~ kosher. They never seem to have problems. Some couples make the other use separate pots or brush their teeth after a meal before they kiss them. If you have no problem with that ~~stupid~~ ritual, you should be fine.

But, seriously, to never be able to eat a cheeseburger? You can still respect that?

My brother has been out of the closet now for most of my adult life. I pretty much deal with it on a "Don't ask, don't tell" basis. Recently, however, he's announced that he's met someone whom he wants to spend the rest of his life with, and they are getting married in California. I don't want to go. I have nothing against my brother, but I can't see him kiss another guy. My wife says that it will insult him, but I think my brother will understand. Do you think it would be terrible if I didn't go to the gay wedding?

You think that your brother wants to see you and *your* wife kiss? Your brother will still be gay whether you go to his wedding or not. Think about how you would feel if he wasn't at yours. If the kissing is what is stopping you, then turn your head and kiss your wife at that moment. And try to be subtle, bigot.

You don't have anything against your brother? How about the fact that your flesh and blood enjoys a penis up his asshole? Do you hold that against him? Your brother likes men's balls in his mouth.

A wedding is one of the most special days in any woman's life, so your brother should love it. Don't be an asshole. The day's not about you anyway. It's about him and his immoral love. Show up, say hi, congratulate him on his happiness, and then go home to your miserable heterosexual family life. It's that easy. In and out. You're back home before your brother and his love are doing a little "in and out" of their own.

I'm talking about them banging each other. Two dudes.

In any case, gay weddings have the best spreads. And by spreads I don't mean how your brother's "groom" spreads his ass cheeks apart so your brother can go deep-ass diving. I mean like they have really good food.

I'm getting married in a few months. I have envisioned my wedding for quite some time and have a lot of the details already set in my head. These details include my wedding party. I picked five of my closest friends to be with me at the altar. What I didn't account for is my fiancé's sister, who is about my age. Am I obligated to put my future sister-in-law in the wedding?

You should have the wedding that you want. It's a day that means a lot to you, and you will remember it always. But if you think it's your day and your day only, then you are sadly mistaken. If you don't want to share the moment, then don't invite anyone. If putting your fiancé's sister in the wedding party will help you get along better with your new "sister for life," then why not make a friend of your future family? Besides, she's one more slave in your entourage whom you can demand things of.

This isn't that big a deal. Let her onstage, and throw her at the end of the line. You get another person to help you get dressed, and later some usher gets her undressed in a broom closet. Win-win.

My wife and I have been married for ten years. We often talk about opening up a little shop somewhere that we can run on our own. We both feel like we might have reached a good point in our lives where this can happen. Is it a mistake to start a business with your spouse?

Of course it's a mistake. Working with your loved one? Work, play, sleep 24/7 with your partner? Yikes . . . familiarity breeds contempt.

Chemda and I can make it work, of course, but we're pretty amazing.

It's important to keep in mind that when you open a business, you no longer work a nine-to-five job. You don't have to clock in anymore, because you're always clocked in. Being your own boss does not mean that you don't have to answer to anyone. You have to answer to your customers, your vendors, the IRS, and each other. When your wife fucks up and forgets to carry the one on your tax return for your new company, will you be able to forgive and have sex with her again? When you don't want to do inventory because you've done it the last couple of times, will you resent her?

Working together happens to work for Keith and me (so far), but we happen to like the positions in our company that we've placed ourselves in. We also enjoy talking shop all the time. The business matches our compatibility. Just remember: It's still work. Also remember to set some time with the two of you where no work is involved.

My fiancé and I are doing all the prep work for our wedding. We understand how registries work, but we already have all the plates, cups, blenders, and the like that we need. We'd like to, instead, register at a bank. We figure the best presents are ones that we can buy for ourselves. Is that uncouth?

People like registries because it saves them time guessing what they should get you. There's no reason registering at a bank, which is possible nowadays, should make anyone feel awkward. You would know how much their normal gift would cost them anyway, so it's not like actual cash makes things weird if they can't spend too much.

Good on ya!

The whole registry thing is awkward, but somehow it became commonplace. It's essentially asking people for gifts. If you found a way to register at a bank, then go for it—society says it's okay.

When I meet people through my husband, he never introduces me with a title. I would like for him to say, "This is my wife, Lucy." Instead he just uses my name sans label. When I talk to him about this he says that he means no disrespect by it, and that most people, if not all, know that he is introducing his wife without him having to announce the fact. I don't see why he just can't add the word that would make me happy. Is there anything I can do to make it happen?

I don't understand why you *need* the title either, but I would do it just to shut you up. It would be very nice of me.

I know you've talked about this with him before, and it seems it's not getting through. How about trying one more time, but this time bring something to the table that he will be happy with? Offer him a change that he's been wanting from you for some time. Tell him that you are willing to exchange his request for yours. Your offer will not only be tempting, but will also show him how much you really need the change.

It's not a big deal to him, but it's a big deal to you, so he should do it. When Chemda introduces me, I like her saying, "This is my Jedi Master Fuck Buddy Supreme, Keith." She could care less either way, but it's important to me, so why not let me have it?

No, don't compromise. Compromise what? That you want to be called "wife"? In exchange he gets a sports car?

Start introducing him as "Chris, the dude that likes to be hog-tied in bed and fucked like a bitch." Then your compromise can be that he calls you his wife, and you call him your husband.

My wedding day is coming. My future wife did all the planning. She's thrown some great parties in her day, so I know that the reception will be a lot of fun. My question is: How much am I allowed to get carried away with the party aspect of it? Normally, I drink. How wasted can I get on my wedding day?

As long as you can fuck her at the end of the night, you're okay.

But like real good.

My husband and I have a unique sense of humor. We are able to poke fun at each other about even the serious things in our lives and still laugh. My problem is when this happens around other people. I feel weird when my husband makes similar jabs in public. I laugh it off, but I feel uncomfortable. Am I being a hypocrite?

Keith and I share a lot on our talk show. We talk about incredibly intimate things that other couples would probably not be okay with sharing with the public. It seems like we have no boundaries, but we do. Everybody has boundaries. You are not being a hypocrite. If he likes being called names during sex, it would not make it okay at a barbecue with your friends for you to ask the Lil' Bitch Pussy Cunt Licker to pass the ketchup. The only reason your husband continues to give himself permission to speak so freely is because you never told him not to.

He'll see the difference if you point it out. Men are going to have fun as much as they can and push everything as far as they can. They're not doing it out of spite, they're doing it because (they think) they can. He was never with a girl like you who jokes around about serious things in private, and he ended up assuming that he had the same permission in public. Tell him the difference, and he'll likely understand.

My husband used to buy me flowers all the time. He would write me letters and buy me small gifts that he came across that made him think of me. Though it's not the only reason I married him, his romantic side definitely played a part. We've been married about five years now, and all of that stuff seems to have faded. He still does special things on Valentine's Day and my birthday, but I miss the smaller, more daily events. Is the romantic side inevitably lost in a marriage?

 Do you still blow him? He remembers a time when he would get one every morning. I bet if you start he'll get that sparkle back in his eye and your romance will begin anew. Don't be lazy if you don't want him to be.

 I know if you blew *me* I'd write you a poem.

My boyfriend and I have been dating for two and a half years. We are both in our early thirties. He recently asked me to move in with him. Am I wasting time doing that? Shouldn't I just get married?

You'd be wasting time if you continued to be with someone who you didn't think was worthy of you. You're not wasting your time spending it with someone you want to be with.

I am a strong believer in living with each other before marriage. It makes sense to know how a person is 24/7 when you start debating about being with them forever.

Talk to your boyfriend about your ideas. See if your future plans match his. Find out if he's even thinking about marriage. I know that women like to be surprised by a wedding proposal, but it's silly not to discuss your future when, in your head, you've already committed to an eternity together.

Wasting time . . . ha jeez.

It's not a contest between your siblings or your friends on who gets married first or who has been married longer. The real contest is who ends up happier. *That's* what you'll enjoy rubbing in their smug faces.

Get to know your man. Learn if he sleepwalks, snores, gets cranky, gets angry, curses at the TV, likes sharing his personal space—everything. Sure, you might feel like you have to keep reminding people how long you've been dating in order to let them know you're the real deal, but unlike those hastily married suckers, you'll be the one who knew her man before they walked down the aisle.

My husband and I have been married for fifteen years now. We were dating five years before that. We are now in our mid-fifties. Our priorities seemed to have changed, and though we love and respect each other, we seem to be wanting more space and time to ourselves. We started talking about having our own bedrooms in our home. We don't use the second bedroom so much right now, so finding space for things is not an issue. We were just wondering if we are overlooking something, and is this a bad idea that will lead to the end of our relationship?

Keith and I brought up the idea of separate bedrooms for couples once on our show. We said it was ridiculous to think that you can sleep in different bedrooms and still consider yourself a happily married couple. We then got a ton of e-mails and phone calls from people who made the decision to have different rooms from their spouses. They cited reasons like their partner's snoring or moving around; they prefer different bed firmness; they have separate sleep schedules due to work, et cetera. It seems the separate rooms helped them stay together.

If you and your husband believe that having separate bedrooms should be your next move, then do it. You know your relationship better than anyone else.

If you both want separate bedrooms because of space and not because you really are starting to despise each other, then enjoy the extra room. You can always go back.

If your husband starts insisting that you knock first, then maybe there's an issue. If he makes you do that, check his computer when he's gone. See what autofills in.

In-Laws

Ahh, yes. In-laws. You finally became an adult—you have a job, you weeded out your asshole friends, you found a nice place to live, and you figured out what's important in life. You take it to the next level with your girlfriend and you say, "I do." You have it all. Little did you know that the wedding chapel was a time travel machine that takes you back to high school—back to the days of bullies making you insecure and more successful people making you feel inadequate. Except now they are called in-laws. But they're still better than you.

I say who cares. I don't need Chemda's parents. They weren't there for me growing up, but her dad still treats me like I owe him something. I get it. I'm with the little angel you raised; I owe you a great debt. Would seven hundred dollars cover it?

People's parents spent money and time and (what they considered) love on their son or daughter, and here you come after all that's done, saying, "I'll take it from here."

"Who the hell are you? Oh, no, it doesn't work like that. You owe me."

"How can I pay you back, in-law? I can't give you all the money or time you spent."

"Oh, I'll find a way."

And then they just make you uncomfortable.

If your relationship is serious, then you can call your significant other's parents "in-laws." You don't have to be married. They already consider you the asshole who's going to ruin their child's life, so you might as well assume they're family. I met Chemda's mother before I met her father. It was awkward, but pleasant enough. The first time I met the father was at Chemda's childhood friend's wedding. We sat at different tables, but at sides that matched up, so if I looked to my right or he to his left, our respective fat heads would be right in the other's face. And yet we never talked, shook hands, or nodded hello. He made it clear through his children he didn't like me because I wasn't Jewish. The one thing he asks of his children is to marry a Jew. After everything he's done for them . . .

I knew sometime during the wedding we'd have to make eye contact. That's when I'd put out my hand. He'd have to shake it.

"Oh, he won't," his children told me.

"He has to. That's the rules."

"You'll see."

I was confused. "So what's he gonna do? Spit on me and leave?"

"You'd be surprised."

As a favor to the rest of his family, I never said hello. The parents since moved back to Israel, and we've never spoken. Chemda and I have never been happier being with each other, and yet the dad has no idea who I am.

When we talked about this on our talk show, the letters came in about how to deal with the dad. Some listeners told me I'd be surprised how nice the dad would be if I just told him how I planned on taking care of his daughter. Others said how I should convert and just make everyone happy. The stupidity flowed in by the shit-ton. People don't understand everyone's not them.

"I have a daughter of my own. I just want her happy with a

man who cares, Keith. You have it all wrong. Just tell her dad how you feel. It's that easy."

Now I just feel bad for the daughter of the guy who wrote that letter. He's an idiot, and she won't be raised properly.

But don't feel bad for me. I feel bad for you. You know your in-laws, and you hate them. They nag and grind and all but physically kick you. More than one person right now, in fact, is reading this and actually has an in-law who kicks them. And still you try to appease. You try so hard because that's what you do. Well, I say, "No more!"

In-laws. Who needs 'em.

"But we're family," they'll exclaim. Just shrug: "Shoulda been nicer."

This dismissal tactic worked with my once Catholic priest father accepting I'm with a Jew, and it'll work on Chemda's father as well. I just have to stand firm. Sand people are more stubborn. If you don't believe me, turn on the news.

IN-LAWS Questions

My wife wants me to go to her parents' house every weekend. How can I get out of it?

The obvious answer is: Just tell her that you don't want to go. What might surprise you is that your wife feels the same way about going to her parents' place all the time. A lot of women tend to do things based on feelings of obligation. Or, instead of telling your wife that you *don't* want to go to her parents' house on Sunday, tell her that you would rather spend a romantic day together. Even if your original idea was to have a day to yourself, this will at least make her think of weekend time differently, and down the line you can make some Saturdays your very own special days.

Everything we as men learned we really *did* learn in kindergarten. How did you get out of story-time? You peed your pants by accident. Then you grew up a little bit and how did you get out of washing the dishes? You broke a few by mistake. Same thing here. "I'm happy to see the in-laws, Chemda. I just sure hope I don't have too much to drink and end up talking inappropriately."

I recently met my future mother-in-law and she is an awful example of a human being. It scared me to death. What are the chances that my future wife will end up this way?

Sometimes, because someone is raised by a certain type of person, they will go out of their way to be the opposite. Your girlfriend may have recognized that her mom's behavior affects people negatively, and she's probably made an effort to act differently herself. Find out what your girlfriend thinks about her mother's unconstructive behavior. It's the best way to see into the future.

My advice is that you get scientific. You need to get the mom angry and see how she reacts, and later you need to get the daughter angry and see how *she* reacts. Then go back to your lab and compare the empirical evidence. Be sure the test is fair, and that they are both getting mad at the exact same thing, such as illegal immigrants. Then see if they use the same words and profane actions. If these two are eerily similar, pack up your science beakers and take the first train to anywhere not there.

My mother is always fighting with my wife. Whose side am I obligated to take?

No brainer: The wife. Your mom stopped making your bed a long time ago

We're in complete agreement. Yes, your mom wiped your ass and paddled you, but your wife is the one who really knows you. Little does your mom know that you *enjoy* being paddled, and that the outfits in the closet aren't all for Halloween. Moms are nice, but eventually we need a new type of caregiver, and we need to keep that person happy.

I'm pregnant with my first child. My mother-in-law wants to be in the room for the birth. This means a great deal to her because this will be her first grandchild. This is not, however, the ideal situation for me. I'm terrified as it is of the delivery process. How do I tell her to stay out without hurting our relationship?

The birth of a child is obviously a big deal—but it's *your* big deal. You should be able to dictate who is in the room with you. I would simply explain that you're extremely nervous and that you prefer that people wait until after the delivery to join you. Remind your mother-in-law that she will, obviously, be a huge part of the baby's life, but that starts at Minute Two instead of Minute One.

Personally, if I gave birth, I'd have it be a party. Balloons, clowns, cotton candy. I'd have my friends waiting by my bottom with catchers' mitts. Caught the baby? That's good luck (old wives' tale). But since only women can give birth, here's what I think you can say: "Sorry, _____, but I'll be nervous if you're there, and I might snap shut during the birth out of fear. Thanks for understanding that I want your new grandkid not to have a squished head."

I'm about to marry the most wonderful man I have ever met. He's great to me and has improved my life to no end. I fear just one thing. His parents are degenerates. They are drug addicts and convicted dealers. I don't see any signs of my fiancé heading in that direction. In fact, he continues to make sure that he resembles nothing of them. Am I naïve?

It sounds like your fiancé's entire life was a scared-straight program. To me, an honest person is a person living honestly. If his parents are great people, that would not necessarily mean that he is a great person. The apple can sometimes be blown away from the tree.

Leave some illegal drugs around his office or some-place that he will find them. Install a hidden cam-era, and follow up on what he does with the drugs.

If what he does is less than savory, kick him to the curb. If he doesn't follow in his family's footsteps, feel better about him, but know that you're a piece of shit. Where did you get drugs anyway?

My wife's mom is mean to her. She puts her down and makes her feel awful every time she sees her. This breaks my heart. Should I interfere?

Chances are that your wife is so used to her mom's abusive tones that she doesn't realize how much it's affecting her life. If you get involved you might end up distancing both your mother-in-law and your wife and creating an even worse relationship between them. If you feel like you have to get involved, then you have to be very gentle about it. In no way are you to point out her mother's flaws. Instead, you have to help her discover the problem on her own. Language like "How did you feel about that?" as opposed to "I re-ally think that your mother was out of line" is crucial. When your wife does start to express that she is not happy with how her mother treats her, don't pounce on that. As soon as you say some-thing negative, her natural instincts will be to take her thoughts back in order to defend her mom. Your role is just to listen and try to get as many of her real feelings out of her as you can. She'll be comfortable calling her mom the C-word in no time . . . and she'll say "C-word." It *is* her mom, after all.

If it's not your place to interfere, then why does your wife keep involving you? Are you supposed to sit there, nod, and realize that her crying is going to happen again and again? Don't include us, ladies, if you don't want us to fix obvious problems.

Tell your wife that by making her sad and angry, her mom is making *you* sad and angry. Tell her that anytime her mom makes her sad, *you* feel helpless and like a loser. Tell her she has to be stronger with her mom or not talk to her as much. How your wife decides to interact with her own mother is up to her until it negatively affects you.

Wow, it's all about you, Keith, isn't it? Didn't know you were so sensitive as to feel the pain of the world. Look at Keith, everybody! Your sadness makes him sad. Don't talk to your mom anymore because it makes Keithy-poo sad in his sad eyes. Oh, Keith.

Wow, what a cunt.

My husband recently told me that he wants his mother to move in. She is no longer able to take care of herself, so it's either our place or a nursing home. His siblings do not have the room in their houses like we do. This is a huge undertaking and a burden I don't wish to take on. I know it sounds selfish, but we have our own life going on with two young kids to take care of, which, to me, is plenty of work. How can I reject his mother without seeming like I'm rejecting him?

You look him sweetly in the eyes, maybe put a hand on his arm to be sure there's a connection, and you say, *"Oh, hells no!"*

What your husband doesn't know is that he doesn't want this undertaking either. It's a bigger burden than he's imagining. He just wants to feel like he's not neglecting the woman who raised him. Have his mom come stay with you guys, but pretend she's a dog that your child wanted. He wants it; he takes care of it. After your husband changes a couple of his mom's diapers, he'll change his tune.

My brother-in-law is one of the biggest jerks I ever met. Unfortunately, he lives close to my husband and me, and he insists on constantly dropping by unannounced. My husband is not thrilled about this notion either, but he allows it because "he's family." Don't I have the right to decide who comes over my house and when, despite its being family?

Start by not having his favorite beer on hand all the time. Don't let him always have the remote. You're making him feel too comfortable in a place where he's not welcome. You have to take some responsibility for why people push your limits. He knows what he can get away with.

Talk to your husband about how often you really want these visits to take place. Make sure to remind him that you both share the same feelings about "family." Express that it's okay for you or your husband to tell the brother-in-law when it's a bad time for a visit because you are in the middle of something personal. Once your in-law has boundaries set, he will respect your space a lot more.

When he's over next time, you need to put kiddie porn on his person or belongings. Then anonymously call the cops.

Sorry, I don't have time for jerks. If this guy's one of the biggest of them: Good-bye.

My mother-in-law keeps telling me that my husband and I should have babies already. We've been married for four years, and we have really been enjoying our life together the way it is. We haven't decided if we will ever have babies, but we know we don't want them now. How do I get my mother-in-law to stop pressuring me to rush into motherhood?

You can't. In the marriage segment I sum up why we all really get married—because we had to be part of someone else's stupid bullshit wedding, and we want to punish them by forcing them to be part of ours. It's our turn! Same thing with moms. Moms had moms who nagged them, and now they have to nag their daughters in return—otherwise, the nag stays in their system like poison—it's very similar to *The Ring*. Pass it on or be destroyed. They will not allow the shit creek of nagging to dam up *their* reservoir.

If it's not about getting married, it's about having kids. If it's not about having kids, it's about having grandkids. Then you get into what schools the kids are going to, what jobs they're getting, et cetera. It never ends. You simply have to ignore your mother or mother-in-law. Just nod, say okay, and move on to the cake course as soon as possible.

You can't make her stop. She's bored. She thinks her son owes her a baby. How do you tell a mom that you are having sex, but for recreational purposes only? You don't. You tell her you're thinking about it, and she'll be one of the first to know if it happens.

My girlfriend's brother is the lead singer in what I think is the worst band I've heard in my life. She's not crazy about the music either, but she feels obligated to go to all his local shows. She drags me along claiming it's the right thing to do. I'm sick of it, and she knows it. How can I get out of going to any more of these events without getting in a fight with her?

Bring headphones. Maybe one of those pocket game systems.

You are not responsible to be the groupies to her brother's band. He has to find fans of his own. That's how these things work. Do you call him to sit in your meetings at work for moral support? I understand going to a couple of the shows once in a while as encouragement. Other than that, she has to pick and choose her outings with you. If it helps, next time you notice a show coming up, plan a nice dinner for the same night and have *her* pick.

My husband's family members are the most competitive people I have ever met. They always have to one-up each other, "win" in conversations, and make everything a life-altering contest. The worst part, for me, is that every time we get together with her family, they have to play board games. They have the worst sportsmanship, and, because of their aggressive play tactics, someone always gets into a fight and feelings are hurt. Our visits never end nicely, and yet they always insist on playing every time we get together. I dread going to their place, and I've faked being sick a couple of times now. I don't want to distance myself from my husband's family, but I feel like they leave me no choice. How do I get my in-laws to socialize without trying to win something?

What's the matter? You can't win one argument? Is Pictionary too hard for you? Are you going to teach your son that there is no winning or losing and why even bother keeping score? You make me sick. You lose at life. Boo.

I know someone with this condition. I won't name names, but it's Chemda. She's the worst. Here's what you need to do: Refuse to play. "Sorry, it's just too much." This is completely their fault, not ours, and they know it. They will behave if you make them, because if they don't behave they have no one to play with. Trust me, it'll work. Again, they already know they're in the wrong. They won't be mad that you pointed it out.

Try Keith's advice. Just expect a competition about who will be the first to convince you to play.

I'm in the kitchen already. I can't hear you.

I've been dating my girlfriend for two years now. We are very serious about our relationship and we both believe that we want to be with each other forever. Our commitment to each other seems to not be enough for her mother. When we've gone up to visit her, she's made us sleep in different rooms. I find this to be ridiculous, as her daughter and I live together already and we are consenting adults who love each other. Should I make a fuss over how I feel or will this cause an issue between my girlfriend and me?

My parents demand the same of me and Chemda when we stay at their place overnight. It's so silly—like we're not gonna just fuck extra when they're not looking. It used to bother me, but I finally shrugged. You're already talking and acting a little different with them, and you're not being the real you anyway. Why not let them have this silliness as well. Who gives a shit? They're gonna die soon. Throw them a bone (and then throw your girl a bone when they're off at church).

Yep, Keith's parents feel the same way when we visit them. We both hate it and have stayed in a hotel a couple of times when in town just so that we can feel more comfortable. Because these are not my parents, I follow Keith's lead. If he wants to say something, then that's on him. If he doesn't, then it's not that big a deal. We're not going over there to hibernate for the winter. It's a short visit. It would be rude of you to decide where to sleep. After all, it is their home.

For the past three years I have been dating a Muslim girl.

Let me stop you right there. *Why?*

Anyway, I am. Now, I was raised Catholic and am now an atheist. Our difference in religion causes no turmoil in our relationship, but her father refuses to acknowledge my existence. I know this hurts her feelings, and it's weird on my end as well. Usually, we just kind of shrug it off and try to keep in mind that this is just a cultural thing. However, I am going to ask her to marry me soon, and I feel like he should somehow be a part of this incredible part of our lives. How do I approach an unapproachable father-in-law?

It's *you* who thinks this marriage is an incredible part of your life. To your girlfriend's father, this is death. What you're doing is asking him to change himself for you to be happy. That's exactly the same as him asking you not to get married because of *his* beliefs. You both have to accept that you cannot get everything you want in this scenario. You have to decide that you are getting married to please yourselves. You can't change anyone's beliefs or politics just because marrying someone is exciting to you.

I say just approach him. What's he gonna do? Kill you? Maybe. I don't know his barbaric ways. But I doubt it.

I ended up meeting Chemda's dad between the time I wrote the opening to this section and the time I'm answering this question, and while I stand by everything I wrote, I still can report this: These guys are extremely nervous and uncomfortable, and they don't have an upper hand at all. In fact, when it comes to you and your lady, you're already in. They don't know if *they* are.

If you want his blessing, say hi. He won't do anything crazy. If his attitude has been too much for you to stomach, then fuck him. That whole asking for a daughter's hand bullshit is outdated, antiquated, and archaic.

My wife and I live in Minnesota, only minutes from my parents' house and the neighborhood where I was raised. This works great for me because I am very close with my family, and I get to see them as often as I want. However, recently, my wife was offered a huge promotion at work. This came with an enormous bonus and a sizable raise. The catch is that we would have to relocate to Wisconsin. This is devastating to me because I feel like I have to choose between my wife's career and my family. I don't want to move. Is it too much to ask my wife to put her career aside for what I want?

Yes, it is. Unless it was discussed ahead of time how you want to forever live in the town you grew up in to be sure you do your part for Minnesota inbreeding, you need to go where your lives will be improved. Not liking the weather of the new place you're moving to is a more valid reason than never wanting to leave Mommy and Daddy. Grow up. There are planes and trains all over the world. You'll see Mommy again.

You're not really choosing between your wife's career and your family. You're choosing between your wife (who is your new family) and your history. Keith is right. Running into Bob from third grade at the Stop & Shop should not be more important than the future you and your wife promised each other.

Christmas is a very big deal in both my husband's and my family, as I'm sure it is in a lot of families. For years, because of the magnitude of Christmas, both our families have been arguing about where and with whom we spend the holidays. The two families live in different states, so it's not possible to visit both families during this time. Every year someone is upset by our decision about Christmas. Is there any way to make both sides of the family feel good about the holiday choices we make?

There is no way to please absolutely everyone. This goes for family Christmases and life in general. The most politically correct way to go about this is to alternate Christmases. Don't ask either side of the family what they think of this. Give them the next ten years' schedule ahead of time, and, if they don't like it, then have Christmas at your place with people you actually like.

Agreed. Tell them you can alternate between the two families every year. Or . . . tell them that you and your husband can flip a coin to see whose house you end up at each Christmas. Maybe your family is the one that wins the most often. Maybe they lose. Either way, each family must have presents ready to give in person.

My in-laws don't speak much English. When my wife and I get together with them, they make an attempt to talk to me for about two minutes, and then they just revert to talking to her only in their native tongue. I end up just sitting there with a silly grin on my face for the rest of the night, as I cannot contribute anything because I have no idea what they're talking about. Should I insist that they speak English, or is a silent dinner my fate?

You can't insist on English. It's not your place, and it doesn't seem like they are capable of it anyway. It sucks for you to be in that position. The most you can ask for is that your wife keep you in the loop by translating here and again. Maybe help out to pass time. Do some dishes, put food out, refill drinks, et cetera. It doesn't sound like fun, but it might be the only way to keep busy. It's also a good way to get on their good side, since they're not happy with the outsider marrying their daughter.

Personally, I'd be fine with this. Let's say I was with Chemda's parents in Israel, and they were speaking Hebrew at the dinner table. I wouldn't fake grin. I'd just eat the food and drink their booze. When Chemda translates, I say, "Don't worry. I'm good." Like I give a shit on how they're remodeling the Wailing Wall by adding extra cracks. If it's important, they'll tell me. Maybe they're talking about me behind my back in front of my face? If they're good about it and I never find out, it doesn't upset me in the least.

Can I still float in the Dead Sea? Yes? Then I'm caught up with everything that's going on in their lives.

I think that most of my wife's family is racist. They talk about other races as if the stereotypes are the only things about them that are true. It makes me feel very uncomfortable. So far I have bitten my tongue about this in their presence, but it's getting tiring, and their ignorance drives me nuts. Would it be a big mistake to speak my mind about this to them?

When I met Chemda's cousins and whatnot in Israel, they constantly made jokes about the death of Arabs. We got stuck in traffic after a car accident, and a family member said that it had better be a dead Arab taking up his time. To me, it felt as inappropriate as me making a snide remark about black people in front of strangers in America, at best. It's weird sometimes to not say something back. I want to tell Chemda's cousin, "God will wipe away all the Arabs? Who do you think made them in the first place?" But what's the point of arguing? I'm not saying we shouldn't try to make the world a better place, but there are times when you have to realize that you're wasting your breath. Debating politics and religion with in-laws is futile. Your "golden words of truth" aren't going to undo a lifetime of racist conditioning. Keep your judgments of your new family between you and your wife (for example, when your wife tells you that her parents thought it was rude that you two left without having coffee, you can ask, "Your racist parents?"); however, outside of that, let it go. Instead, let Christ Jesus judge them at the gates of Heaven. I mean, I know you believe that Jesus Christ is the one true savior. I don't think that's even debatable.

Talk to your wife about how you feel about this. Maybe she's been waiting for someone to help whale on them for some time. Together you can tag team the family. Bring a steel ladder, cage-match style.

My brother-in-law recently asked to borrow a large sum of money. My wife and I live off some wealth that I made during the dot-com boom. Though we are not incredibly rich, the money covers our middle-class lives without our having to work. I can spare the money, but I don't think he's capable of returning it. I don't want to cause a rift in the family, but does that mean I have to lend the money?

It is not an obligation to lend relatives money. In fact, many people have a policy specifically against money and family mixing. If you think that this guy is a bad risk, then you do not have to give him anything. You worked hard for what you have, and he needs to work too. If your wife gives you grief about it, tell her that she can lend her brother the money from her allotted allowance. I think that will change her tune.

Mo' money, mo' problems.

Chemda's idea is perfect. Remind your wife that you made a lot of money because you're smart and able to judge things, and putting your money at risk could change your lives for the worse. When it comes to money, you have to think with your head, not your heart.

I'm an accountant. Around April, my in-laws start contacting me in panic about their taxes. This is obviously a time when I am swamped with my own clients. They seem to not understand that I can't just drop my business to answer every question that they obviously didn't even bother looking up before calling me. I don't mind helping. I just want them to be mindful of my time. Am I asking for too much?

You're not asking for too much. They are. They're asking you to put your life on hold because they've neglected their obligations. If you really don't mind helping them, then warn them ahead of time about your schedule. Tell them in January that you have some time in February to help them out. Give them a time period that fits your schedule, and warn them that after that date you will be swamped. If they still call you in April, then you and/or your secretary will have to say that you are too busy to take their call. If they can't understand that, then I guess you lost them as friends. Boo fuckin' hoo.

What do they do for a living? Ask them information about that, all the time. Are they a doctor? Keep calling them about a cough or a new lump. Are they a janitor? Dial them up anytime there's a spill to ask what cleaning agent is best. I'm not a fan of passive-aggressiveness, but I am a fan of aggressive aggressiveness. Let them understand it's a two-way street.

My girlfriend and I are getting married in a few months. Her dad offered me a position in his company after we marry. If I take the job, I will be making more money and my wife won't have to work. My problem is that I will be working for my father-in-law. It's not like I hate the guy. I just don't know if I want my in-laws to be part of my day-to-day life, and I feel awkward having to rely on my wife's father for my position. Is it smart to take the job, or should I turn it down?

Take the job. It sounds like you're not even qualified for it, and yet he's paying you double what you make now just for marrying his daughter. If your other job is something that you have been working for and trying to build a future with, that's a different story. It sounds, though, like a job is a job to you, so you might as well take the position that helps you with your new family.

Have your wife take the job, and you relax. They're already family, and they'll get along easier than you and he ever will. I say you propose this idea to her dad before you propose it to her so that it's a nice surprise and she doesn't feel like she was handed a gimme.

Extra-Relationship Affairs

Here we go. Affairs. If you're reading this book out loud with a loved one, feel free to skip this segment and move on to the next. You can come back to this in privacy to not stir up any bad feelings. If the editors moved this segment to the end, set yourself on fire. For a lot of you, self-immolation will be a lot easier than reading this aloud. This one can get a little dicey.

Anytime I see a movie or hear a radio conversation about a couple cheating or being caught cheating, I think of all the millions and millions of people who have cheated and all the shows and conversations they've heard in front of the ones they've cheated on and how uncomfortable that must have been. How many good films can't be watched with your mate anymore? You're flipping through the channels with the wife you cheated on, happy you were able to work out your rough patch, and you see a married Michael Douglas fucking a hot, single Glenn Close on a countertop after flirting at a party in *Fatal Attraction*. Awkward!

"Do I switch the channel? Oh, God, I know she knows this movie. Everyone knows this movie. How can't she know this movie? I was flipping the channels and it came on. I can keep flipping, I guess, like a sex scene on TV is all of a sudden of no interest to me. Or do I just play it? We said we're fine now, didn't we? Think, me, think." A second hasn't even gone by yet. "She has to know I've stalled too long on this channel. Oh man . . . why did I have to bang that girl at work on her countertop? It could have been anywhere, but no. I had to get caught on a countertop. Maybe I can distract her by cooking dinner with her. She said she wanted to make lasagna together. I'll just turn off the TV and ask if she wants to cook with me. We'll go right into the kitchen together. Shit, there's a counter-top in there too . . . I better just go get the gas and matches now."

Chemda and I have never cheated on each other, for the record (at least as of press time) and the main reason, at least for me, isn't even out of respect. It's so I can flip through the radio or randomly pick out a movie without fear.

But most people have cheated. That's just the way of the world. I see it all the time with friends and coworkers. Chris Rock said, "You're only as faithful as your options," and all the guys and girls in the audience, all in committed relationships, mind you, laughed and nodded. Then they went home together never to bring up the point again.

If you picked up this book in the relationship section of your bookstore, then you already know about all the silly books out there like *Why Men Cheat* and *Why Boys Stray*. These are actual books. With pages. With words on them. Remember the Pet Rock? A man made millions of dollars selling nothing but a rock—a plain rock—by calling it a "pet." Well, I firmly believe the rock was more helpful to people than these dumb books. I guess it's hard to get a book deal based on the proposal "Men cheat because they like other vaginas too."

"Alright, and how will you break that down into separate chapters?"

"Into separate huh?"

Women have to tell themselves it can't be that simple. They need some bullshit philosophy or else they'll think they're losing it. But it is that simple. The person he cheated on you with is not you. That's all there is to it. So now the questions are: What can you do about it? Should I set his iPhone to trail him? Should I get a new face and see if I can seduce him away from myself? We'll tackle all these questions below, of course. But let me say first, it's not just men cheating on women. Wipe that smug look off your face, whore. They say (you know these yappers) 60 percent of men and 40 percent of women cheat in a marriage. (I think it's safe to assume the numbers are higher outside of an oh-so-sacred marriage.) Sixty percent of men and 40 percent of women. I think we can meet in the middle and say it's 50 percent for both. After all, a guy counts flirting and kissing a stranger cheating, whereas it seems like a woman doesn't think that she's cheating unless her heart's involved and there was talk about moving to Cancún forever. Blow jobs don't count. Christ, women don't count "Everything But" as cheating. I always thought that meant everything but sex. They say it does, but it really means *EVERY SINGLE LITTLE THING* But. These single little things include making out, fingering, and even oral . . . A lot of women count ass-fucking as still Everything But.

Fuck it, I'm raising you bitches to 80 percent.

So what's the point? I don't know. I'm really asking. What *is* the point?

Are we always to assume that we will get cheated on? Is this something that we should do ourselves since it's inevitable that someone will do it to us? "Human behavior" or not, no one is okay with someone lying to them—not even people who lie all the time. So, what *are* we supposed to do? Trust or leave. You have to let that person live, and you have to trust that he/she will make the right decisions. Tracing, reading e-mails, and the like will only lead to paranoia and the death of the relationship. You either are in it for real or you're not in it at all. Plus, it's amazing how much you can get to know a person. Most of the time, I can tell something is wrong by the slightest change in Keith's face. So, Keith, I'll know. Just keep that in mind.

God, you're smart. Let's go bang on the countertop.

EXTRA-RELATIONSHIP AFFAIRS
Questions

I cheated on my girlfriend. How do I tell her?

If you're going to tell her that you cheated but then break up with her anyway, don't bother coming clean. What's the point? You'll only be hurting her feelings and hurting her ability to trust the next person.

There seems to be no other way to tell someone that you fucked up other than just telling them. Trying to butter up the situation by doing something like taking her out to dinner will only taint your integrity. You're about to hurt someone who trusts you. Be humble, be a good listener, and be quick with your reflexes. There might be some sharp items flying your way.

You *scuuuuum* . . .

It's not the affair that gets me, it's that your question is "How do I tell her?" You knew it was wrong when you did it, you did it anyway, and every day that goes by makes you feel like a piece of shit. *You* need peace? She doesn't need to know. She didn't do anything wrong, so why does she need her world turned upside down? You're doing this for you. Well, I say, fuck you. Live with yourself.

Wow, Keith! You wouldn't tell me? Good to know.

But know that the pain I'm holding inside hurts daily.

Mine too. ;)

Is it okay to stay with a man after he cheats on you?

We've decided that well over half the world has cheated. And those are people who are admitting it. If you think you can trust the guy again, then I say go for it, meaning, don't break up with him because of the way you think the world will judge you. The world is busy being bent over a stranger's car right now. Only you can say if you trust this person anymore. And don't stay together for kids or any silliness like that. You believe it was a onetime thing or you don't.

Staying in a relationship after someone cheated on you can feel like you are condoning what they did to you. It's not a decision that anyone can help you with. You have to weigh the pros and cons and think about the pain of the affair versus the loss of the relationship. I don't think that it's possible to continue a healthy relationship without going through a very hard time together that involves really laying your emotions on the table. For most, therapy is a must.

And therapy should be paid for by his personal checking account, not your joint checking account.

My boyfriend joined the military and is being shipped off for an unknown amount of time. I'm young and want to move on. Am I a bad person?

You're not a bad person. You just don't love your country all that much. You should not have to feel forced into a commitment because someone else decided to obligate their time to something they are interested in. It's better to let him know before he ships off so that he doesn't come back to a surprising situation.

Chemda's right. The relationship wouldn't have survived anyway. And don't feel guilty when he comes back in whatever horrendous condition he's in after trying to make America a better place for you and your future family.

Is it okay to follow the rule: "What happens in Vegas stays in Vegas"?

That's a commercial, ya dummy! Do you also believe that you, too, can have abs of steel if you only devote five minutes a day?

Don't ask me, ask your Mrs. Butterworth's syrup bottle the next time she comes to life over breakfast.

I'm concerned that my spouse is cheating. Is there a subtle way of finding out?

There are ways that seem subtle but end up dangerous. You can check his computer, his phone, his pants pocket, et cetera. You can turn yourself into what you think is the greatest detective ever, but what you're really doing is driving yourself crazy. You'll read into things a bit too much, you'll be acting very suspicious, and when you do or don't find something, the end result is that you cheated *his* trust to get what you wanted.

Here's what I do as a detective. Let's say you think your girl is messing around with a guy named Mike. When the two of you are doing something random—say, getting the dirty clothes together— ask her in a normal tone, "You like fucking Mike?" Judge if she looks confused or insanely nervous, but understand this isn't an admission either way, so cover up with "I said, I think I dress like a dyke," and point out the bad flannel in your wardrobe. Do this a few times with different responses in the next couple of days, such as, "I said, do you like to hike," or, "I said, I'm not a fan of Hitler's Third Reich." If her head explodes within the week, she was cheating.

Is it wrong to read my spouse's e-mail?

If you're coming from a bad place, such as spying on a loved one, then it's wrong.

No, it's not okay. Are you reading this book out of order?

I recently started thinking of a coworker while having sex with my husband. I thought it would be a onetime thing, but I find myself doing it every time now. Is this cheating?

"Cheating" is a strong word and should be reserved for things that are your fault. If you're being appropriate at work, you're not doing anything wrong. You can't help what gets in your head. With that said, you may have something new to think about: Would you rather be with your office pal instead of your husband? Chances are you wouldn't, so enjoy the brain accidents when they happen.

There are no thought police here. Did you ever think that you wanted to choke the hell out of your boss? Nobody arrested you for that, right?

I find my best friend's boyfriend very attractive. What do I do?

What do you do about what? What are your options here? Look up the words *best friend* and *boyfriend*. Decide if you're a jerk or not.

Let her sleep with your boyfriend and she'll let you sleep with hers. That's what best friends do, right? Then make out with her a little bit. Send pictures to KeithLovesLesbians@KATG.com.

My wife recently started talking about her being with another woman. I know that a lot of guys find it hot for a woman—even their own woman—to be with another lady, but I can't help but feel some jealousy when the subject is brought up. If I'm already having issues with this and nothing has happened yet, I don't think that I can handle her actually going through it. How can I avoid this without looking like a sissy and without her feeling unfulfilled?

Did she tell you that she was bisexual early on in the relationship? That would be the time to let you know what does and doesn't complete her when it comes to being monogamous. If she's springing this on you now, then let her know that you forgot to tell her that you are a polygamist and a sex addict. No need for you both to go unfulfilled.

Have you seen lesbian porn? I get your point, but watch some lesbian porn. I'm on your side completely about her staying faithful. Are you two exclusive or not? However, not for nothin', I recommend you watch some lesbian porn.

I've been dating someone for about a year and a half. She's told me that she has cheated on everyone else whom she's dated in the past. This only made me paranoid. I feel like she's prone to cheating, and that eventually she will just do it to me as well. Am I being unreasonable?

You are not being unreasonable. If someone told you that they never pay back what they borrow, would you lend them money? She is telling you her emotional credit history, and it's not good. Her past does not make it inevitable that she will cheat on you, but you have to decide if you think she is trustworthy or not. If you look over your shoulder your entire relationship, it might not be worthwhile. It's on you now to decide if you trust her or not.

Will she cheat on you? Hold on, let me ask her.

My wife and I have recently separated. We're not sure yet if this will lead to divorce or not. Is it cheating if I am now physically intimate with other people?

It's up to the rules you made. And if you didn't make any, make them. Be clear about what you'll be doing. Sure, part of it's sad, but you're also in an exciting, unique situation where you can be yourself and see if, being an older, more experienced You, you still want to live the life you used to. Don't lie about anything now. You may not get such a fantastic opportunity again.

Tell her, then fuck away.

Just like there are rules to marriage, dating, and divorce, there are rules to separation. Everyone has their own set of guidelines for every part of their life. Why guess at this? If you're uncomfortable asking her directly, then tell her that you are looking to talk over the general strategy of the separation. Come with a list of debatable aspects of a separation that you compiled through Internet searches of other people's concerns during their separation. The list, which will include your question, will seem less personal, so it won't hurt feelings as easily. With this, you will get your answer and probably score points for the research you did.

I've been married for about five years. My wife is a bit possessive, which I understand is how women are when you're married. Small things set her off. For example, if I tell her that I'm having lunch with a female coworker, I get shit for days. This led me to have secret (nonsexual) relationships with the opposite sex. I have two female friends whom my wife never met. I never did anything inappropriate with them and I see them rarely, but I really enjoy their company. I feel like if I tell my wife about any female relationship, she will flip. Am I cheating?

Are you cheating? No. Are you lying? Yes. But it's your wife's fault.

When I know I'm 100 percent right, and I've said my piece, no one can make me feel bad. I won't give credence to any bitching. You say: "I have friends who are women. I'm not cheating. Nothing weird is happening. That's the end of it." Ignore her bitching. Don't apologize to make it go away, and don't nod your head in agreement like you understand. You don't understand. She's out of line, and she's making herself and other women look stupid. Eventually she'll drop it because she has to.

If it was Keith hiding these relationships, I'd be pissed. And let's face it, if you found out she was doing the same, you'd be pissed too. You never put your foot down about this, and now you act as if your wife is making you lie to her. Stand your ground or you're setting a precedent for yourself that every time you make your wife uncomfortable, she will bully you into lying. Are you cheating? You're cheating your relationship.

My wife's best friend is gay. My issue with this is that they are very physically affectionate with each other. I know that he's not sexually attracted to women, but it feels odd when I walk into my living room and they're spooning on the couch. Am I too much of a prude?

Girls tend to be more physically intimate with each other without it being sexual. A lot of women put their gay friends into this category as well. They don't feel threatened by the physical touches of a gay man, so they trust being close without it meaning anything sexual. However, if you feel like a specific act is something too intimate for your wife to share with another person, then that's how you feel.

You're not in the wrong. It's weird that gay men believe they can do whatever they want to women sexually—grab their breasts, kiss their mouth, spoon with a hard-on—because they're not attracted to women. I don't like dudes, but it doesn't make it a cute joke if I teabag any of my buddies.

Tell her you don't like it. She's yours, not the gay community's.

I'm dating a girl who is super paranoid that I will cheat on her. She checks up on me all the time and accuses me of things I wasn't even close to being a part of. I've never given her reason to believe that I would be unfaithful. She just assumes that men are untrue to their women because her father was untrue to her mother. How can I possibly change her mind about that?

Her dad also made a hell of a potato-leek soup. Does she expect you to also?

Break up with her till she gets her shit together. There's nothing you can do.

As Keith said so eloquently, this is not on you to fix. Daddy issues are something that she needs to deal with with her daddy or with her therapist. If she can't trust a guy, then, when you're trying to convince her otherwise, she won't believe you anyway. You're the enemy, and you can't win.

My wife of twelve years suggested that, for the first time in our relationship, we take separate vacations. Is this cause for concern?

Time apart is good for a relationship sometimes. Maybe she wants to be with her girlfriends so nobody sighs at her when she takes too long looking at the local flowers and discussing their color and origin. Maybe she wants to go antiquing all day long without someone rolling his eyes. This could be good for you. Go hunting with your friends. Go adjust your balls with no judgments at a baseball game with your buddies. Though you are together for a reason, your wife and you can't possibly have all the same interests or want to be around each other every single moment of your lives. It's okay to have a good time without each other.

You don't want to be with me every minute of your life? What the who?

I've been married for ten years. My wife is great, and our relationship has been working through even the hard times. Recently, an ex of mine contacted me saying she will be in town for the weekend. This happens to be a weekend that my wife will be out of town. I love my wife, but the idea of sleeping with someone without her finding out seems harmless and fun. If I know I can get away with it, should I go with the ol' "What she doesn't know won't kill her"?

Why not? While she's away, what you don't know won't kill *you* either. Right?

There's no such thing as a guarantee to not be caught. Your ex might get weird on you and threaten to tell. You might get her pregnant. She might leave something behind. You never know. I don't think that being caught should be the reason not to cheat, but since you seem to think so, all I can tell you is that this can cost you your "great wife" and the relationship that has been working well so far.

It's not worth it. These bitches today can't keep a secret. She'll send you cute texts that hint that you both were fucking; you'll get some panties in the mail—all sorts of silliness. There are too many women empowerment movies and songs that keep these whores from shutting their yappers. If the ex thinks you should be with her instead of your wife, she might think that she's doing you a favor by blowing up your spot. Forget it. Still have fun while the wife's away. Play Call of Duty wearing her panties and huffing down whippets—shit like that. But banging an ex is too much when things are going well.

When things are going bad, sure, hire a prostitute. But only bang an ex when you're willing to understand that it will all end at home.

I recently caught my wife cheating on me. I came home early and she didn't see me while she was with another man in our home. This is devastating to me. We've been married for seven years and I thought everything was great. I haven't told her that I know about the affair because I don't know how to approach this at all. What do I do now?

First of all, good for you that you were able to keep your cool from the time you sent this letter in to the time your answer got published. It's over a yearlong process, and you were able to stay calm? Good self-control! I bet it happened again, didn't it?

I've debated about what I'd do if that happened to me. Do I punch heads right there, or do I walk away like you did and plot revenge?

I'd like to think I'm a mature person and that'd I'd plot revenge.

How it must tear you apart to see her smile at you after you know—to hear her, unprompted, tell you how much she loves you. This bitch . . .

Start the process with a lawyer now. You can always rescind your divorce or demand of settlement if you work through it, but be sure you're the first to have things drawn up. It's like being the first to call the police after a fight. You'll have a leg up. Second, throw up some video cameras if the law allows. Get proof for the court case. Start printing out copies of her e-mail and phone records. Then, if you decide to go through with the divorce one day, do it in a fun way. Let's say you're arguing over the TV. You want to watch *SportsCenter*, and she wants a repeat of *Sex and the City*. Say, "Is it okay, though, if I watch this now, because they repeat your show even more often than mine, and you fucked Bob in our bed again last Thursday?" Stare at her as she gasps for air, then go and get your packed bags and leave for the already-paid-for hotel.

In the meantime, when she's gone this weekend, feel free to bang your ex.

 I'd like to do what Keith suggested, but if I ever caught Keith cheating on me, the sounds of me puking in the bathroom would give away that I'm there. My stomach responds without me wanting it to. I don't know how you walked away, but I'm sure it wasn't easy. It sounds like you have a strong stomach, so I say follow

Keith's advice. While you're at it, during the time you're making your plans, watch movies with her that are based on couples who cheat. Watch her squirm.

My high school sweetheart recently contacted me through an online social networking site. We've since been catching up and reminiscing via e-mail here and there. My wife thinks that this is cheating even though all of our communication has been completely platonic. If it matters, my friend is married as well. I feel like I'm not doing anything wrong. Am I missing something?

 Your wife is not necessarily scared that you will cheat on her. She might be thinking that she's missing out on the fun that you guys are having. She wants to be a part of what you're sharing with this woman even though she will not relate to the specifics. She's scared that she will lose you to this woman emotionally, since fresh people in your life can seem a lot more fun and easier to hang out with than a person you have to do serious things with, like figuring out finances.

 Fill your wife in on everything you and your new (old) friend talk about. I mean everything. Talk about the old football team, the crazy stoner, that bitch Mrs. Lattuch—every little insignificant thing that only makes sense if you were there. Bore the shit out of her. After about two or three times of this, your wife will stop worrying, and she'll stop asking silly questions.

My girlfriend has a close male friend whom she spends a lot of time with. Should I be concerned about their meetings?

I have a couple of close male friends, and I know other women who do as well. To us, it's not weird. We don't consider the gender of the friend. We just know we like hanging out with them. I know that I'm lucky that Keith is not a jealous guy. Most men would probably give me shit for my relationships, but it's something that I can't really change. I have no bad intentions when I hang out with either male or female friends, though I know that Keith wouldn't mind some naughty intentions with the womenfolk. Oh, Keith . . .

All my buddies think it's weird that Chemda spends a lot of time with guy friends, but I'm okay with it. Then again, I'm New School. I've evolved. It's about trust, and if there was shadiness going on, I think Chemda would be far more subtle. Plus the dudes she likes are all fruits. I can tell.

My girlfriend doesn't always know that she's being hit on. She even gets hit on by some of her male friends sometimes. When I tell her this, she laughs and says that it's all in my head. I know how men work, and it's definitely happening. Is she retarded?

Huh? I don't understand the question.

Chemda's like this. I know the friends she has, though, and they know if they were inappropriate they'd get a claw hammer through their face, so I'm okay with them. But otherwise, some days Chemda will come home and mention a fellow musician who gave her a shoulder rub or a bartender who wants to take her ice skating (an activity that I don't enjoy). It's always a surprise to her when I say that these people, whom I also know, are trying to get in her pants. Sometimes women are just naïve, or they like to pretend they're naïve, and they don't see the big picture.

Chemda will start to make plans with some new guy she just met who seems cool, and she'll happen to throw something out about me such as "My boyfriend might have the car. When *are* the museum times?" and—surprise, surprise—the trip to the museum might not work out after all. Even then she usually doesn't put it together.

Men are scum, and women need to understand this. The sooner they do, the less time they will live life being sad every time they feel used. All you can do is to sit her down and explain the updated version of the birds and the bees: "Men love pussy. They will do anything to get it. The End."

Is it sad that women have to be on guard like this all of the time? Yes, it's a shame. But that's the way it is. She only has to remember how the two of you met.

Kids

We cover all kinds of advice questions on our show, but some of the most controversial topics are when we tell parents how to make their relationship work better with their children. We cover everything from how to treat a spouse who's having or just had the child to where couples are going wrong in raising their kids. Like political discussions, our beliefs on how to raise a child are welcomed and honored by the listeners who hold the same point of view. The letters and phone calls of praise pour in. If we disagree with a listener's point of view about their child-rearing abilities, however, we are idiot mouthy fuckin' know-nothings who don't have kids and can't possibly know what it's like. Recently, we lost a listener because we told her that if her kid is eating too much candy at home, then she and her husband should limit the child's candy intake at home. She felt attacked, and after listening to the show intently for three years—and thoroughly enjoying it—we may now proceed to go and fuck ourselves in Hell.

I'm sorry, but God gave us the gift of good judgment, and to not use it on your behalf because of potential hate backlash would be nothing short of a moral crime. We know the answers to kid questions, and we're going to help fix your issues. If this disgusts you as a parent, feel free to close the book now. If you want the truth from an outsider who's not blinded by your child's smile, laugh, and charm, then we're the ones who can finally help. We're not worn out in the brain from midnight feedings or teenage angst. Our heads are still together.

To bring up the political analogy again, can someone have an opinion on the government without living in the White House? Of course they can.

Just because we haven't had kids ourselves, that doesn't mean we haven't experienced yours. And they're fuckin' assholes, so pay attention.

KIDS Questions

My husband is constantly handing out money to our kids. Every time they go anywhere, he gives them some cash without thinking that the money is adding up to more than a child needs. I don't want to deprive my kids of going out with their friends to things like the movies and arcade, but I think a limit should be set. How can I not be the bad guy in this scenario?

The answer, since you want them to have some money, is an allowance. The child learns about responsibility, realizes the prices of things, and starts saving for bigger items or events. As a parent, your husband needs to agree that he can't cave if the money is mismanaged, no matter how many times these kids bat their eyelashes.

Personally, I never got a allowance. Now Chemda handles all the money as, apparently, I know nothing.

While you are introducing an allowance, introduce chores as well. Don't make every chore equivalent to a dollar amount, because then they will misunderstand and think that they're doing you a favor by doing something simple, like taking out the garbage. They will also think that they have the option to not do the duties they despise, believing that they can pass on that dollar amount for the week. Instead, tell them what needs to be done by the end of the day or week, and, if it's not done, then their privileges (that includes not only allowance but TV, computer, phone, et cetera) will be taken away.

My husband and I have different views on disciplining our future child. I believe in talking, time-outs, and taking privileges away. He believes in spankings and beatings depending on their age. Which one of us is right?

Ask people you know—ones with good attitudes and ones with bad attitudes—how they were raised. Was punishment physical when the child was out of line, or, were they sent to their room? More often than not, you will find out that the people you respect were hit when they were punished as a kid.

I see how you snuck in the word *beatings*. Your husband didn't say "beatings." He said "spankings." *Misleading the court, Your Honor!* I believe spankings are necessary. It can't be debated about what's more effective—spankings, being made to feel guilty with words, or loss of privileges—because whatever you received as a kid, you think is the most effective. I can tell you this, though: If all I'd gotten for acting up as a child was a talking to or ten minutes in the time-out chair, I would have walked all over my parents and ruled the roost.

Try it your way first. When you see that doesn't work, a few hits should calm them down.

Keith and I have similar disagreements. I don't believe that you should hit a child. I think that shows loss of temper, lack of ability to express oneself, and it leads to a diminished respect between you and the child. This is not to say that I think children need to be babied and that their opinion should be held in the same regard as the parents'; however, if you teach kids that when you're so mad you have to hit, they will mimic that. Hitting also gets old. Once a child reaches an age where they are stronger, your spanking sessions are no longer apt. You'll then have to find another way of disciplining, and at that point it becomes difficult to introduce something new.

I don't think hitting a child shows a lack of control. My physical punishments were always after a talk about what I'd done wrong. They were drawn out, also. I had to go and get my own wooden spoon to get hit in the ass with. There wasn't a loss of self-control. There was *plenty* of control.

Start with words, when that fails go with loss of privileges, and when that fails, go to fisticuffs. It's up to the child how far he or she wants to take it. Some kids need to be smacked.

For the record, I was never hit as a child.

No duh.

My husband keeps speaking French to our kid. We live in the United States, and I don't speak any French. I'm afraid that my child will not be able to converse with anyone because he will only be speaking French. Will he be behind in school?

My first language was Hebrew. We moved to the United States when I was four and a half. I didn't speak a word of English, and neither did my parents.

Children learn languages very easily. As soon as my parents put me in an English-speaking environment, I was speaking English. I am now bilingual, which I definitely would not be if I hadn't learned Hebrew when I was a child. As far as my English: I wrote a book!

These kids pick up things quickly and easily in any environment. You know it's true when your child repeats how she heard from you that "Nana is a cheap bitch" at the Christmas dinner table. Oh, the mouths of babes . . .

It's smart what he's doing. Your only worry is that one day they'll turn on you, and you'll have no idea what either of them are saying. *Sacré bleu!*

My wife and I can afford a nanny, but my wife is a stay-at-home mom. Why should we include a stranger in our child's life when his mom is around all the time?

Though it's not impossible to raise a child without a nanny—or a husband for that matter—it's nice to have extra hands to help. Think of being at home with the child as a job. When you're working, you get a lunch break, a cigarette break, time to yourself in the bathroom, and even a workout if you choose. Moms at home don't have these luxuries. For example, they have to take the kid with them in the bathroom, depending on the child's age.

She never *needed* flowers, but you knew to get those. Have a nanny come for a couple of hours a day. It will give your wife a break to be an adult and not simply a mommy machine. Who knows, she might take part of that time to work out. Isn't that nice?

 If you needed a secretary at work and her salary affected the money you were bringing home, you'd still hire one because of how much it helps the workload. Can you work without a secretary? Probably. The company may suffer, but it probably won't. Same with your wife. She can use the help. Can she take care of the baby without the nanny? Probably. She may lose her shit one day and shove the baby in the microwave and cook it for five minutes, but she probably won't.

My girlfriend is getting on the pill. I'm happy to be rid of condoms, but how can I be sure she's taking it properly?

 You can't always be there to put the pill in her mouth. You have to trust that she cares enough about not messing with her own body's system that she's taking the pill regularly.

I set my phone alarm to the time I need to take the pill. I also set Keith's alarm to ring an hour after, just in case I flaked. Feel free to use my idea. Don't tell her that it's because you think she's flaky. Tell her that you want to be involved since she's doing this nice thing for the two of you.

If it's a trust issue, don't trust her if you have doubts. But to be honest, if she wanted to trick you she could have already been poking holes in your condoms.

By the way, you're going to like her pussy so much better. Now you're actually fucking it.

I just found out that I'm pregnant. We decided to tell people right away. My husband keeps announcing that *we're* pregnant. It drives me nuts. Does he have any right to say that?

The "we're pregnant" thing drives everyone crazy. I think it started as some kind of stupid women's movement thing to involve men and let them know that they, too, are part of the process. Well, they clearly are not.

Tell your husband that you don't like when he says that he's pregnant. I bet he'll be relieved. He was probably feeling stupid and only saying it because he thought you wanted him to.

"We're pregnant" sounds weird to my ears too. I would never say it if Chemda was pregnant. Like Chemda said, he could be doing it because he's hearing everyone else do it, and maybe he thinks it will please you. However, he could be saying that you're both pregnant because he's trying to be part of the whole experience.

227

Tell him you find it stupid when he says, "We're pregnant," but be sure you don't take all his excitement away.

A lot of women don't give their husbands any credit when they're pregnant or dealing with a newborn because the mom does so much the man can't do, such as hold the baby in his womb, breast-feed the baby, et cetera; but, there probably are many things the man is doing, not to mention dealing with your hormonal mess and keeping you from ironing the baby's face in a fit of rage.

Recognize where the sperm came from, and acknowledge that he's in this with you. Girl Power is a great thing, but maybe he'd like to feel some joy too.

I am a single guy in my mid-twenties. I've been dating for a while, but now it seems that women my age are starting to take dating a bit more seriously. They want to know that there is a future and purpose to us being together. At what point in the relationship do I need to tell them that I do not ever want kids?

Say it whenever you want. No one will believe you. Women have a tendency to think that they can change a guy, and they can't believe that someone doesn't want a precious baby of their own. I've been saying that I don't want a baby for years, and I still get people telling me that something in my brain will kick in. Everyone knows that I won't be able to resist putting my uterus to work. I still have no child and I still don't ever want one.

She sure is going to feel awkward that this was in print when we have our baby . . .

My wife is pregnant. We just found out it's a girl. I really wanted a boy, and I'm a little disappointed. Does that make me a bad person?

It doesn't make you a bad person, but you may want to keep your gender wish to yourself. People tend to judge and never forget that kind of information.

I think a lot of people feel the same way as you, but they aren't admitting it. It's okay to have a preference, and it's okay to be a little disappointed; just don't make a big deal out of it or name the girl Dan.

We live in the future now. See if the doctor can fix it in the womb for an extra two hundred dollars or so. If not, maybe she'll at least be a dyke.

My wife and I were both raised Catholic, but are now nonbelievers. We're going to have a baby and started considering celebrating some of the Catholic holidays. This would be for family and for tradition's sake. Are we being hypocrites?

I was raised Jewish, turned atheist, and celebrate the different holidays of my friends and family. Celebrating by eating together and coloring in fictional characters does not a religion make. This is one of the times where, I believe, intent is everything. When I make Christmas dinner for friends or go to church with Keith's family on Easter Sunday, I am honoring what they believe. My excitement for the holiday comes from people getting together and feeling good. If you want your child to experience that, then go for it.

When it comes to keeping traditions like coloring eggs and exchanging presents on Christmas, then by all means have a good time. It's fun. But skip church. You're done.

If you still have some believer residue left over, and you wonder if you should take your kids to church "just in case," look at it this way: Your kids can only commit a sin if they do so knowingly. If they don't know things are sinful, they do not get punished for it by God. If you ask me, it's a *disservice* to give them the knowledge that can assure them eternal damnation. Do them and yourself a favor, and enjoy the free time together as a family that church would have otherwise taken up. Explain to them that stealing is a crime, but when they ask if it's a sin, shrug and say, "No one knows."

My wife is breastfeeding. I can't help but be curious about what it tastes and feels like to drink from her breast. Would it be out of line to ask?

I can't help it either. Can I have a taste?

That's not out of line in the least. Sincerely. It's there. You've both done much worse together. Enjoy.

If she says anything like "That's weird," explain to her what weird is.

"I had my penis inside you," you can remind her. "The part of my body that I urinate with was inside your mouth! That's what's weird. This is just milk."

I'm thinking of getting pregnant. I would, of course, be giving up drinking, smoking, and whatever else is on the list of things to avoid. I think it's a bit unfair for me to be alone in this, since this is my husband's baby too. Is it too much for me to ask him to give up all the things I'm giving up while I'm pregnant?

Is it dumb when a guy says, "We're pregnant"?

After reading this question, I started asking myself if I would want Keith to follow my regimen if I were pregnant. The response that I wanted to have was: No way. It's my pregnancy, and I will be responsible for it. However, when I thought about what a twenty-four-hour, seven-day-a-week job being with child would be for nine to ten months, I started thinking about how I would be alone at home while he was out partying. I thought about how I would be going through a lot of pain carrying the child, such as morning sickness days and body changes. The baby would be taking everything from me. I started thinking that it wouldn't kill Keith to stop the things he is enjoying for me. After all, I'm going through this for us and the baby.

The truth that I can't ignore is that Keith would not be the one pregnant. I have to be aware that he will be going through his own things in anticipation and preparation. In reality, no matter how you look at it, the burden of being pregnant is on a woman. That includes the baby's health relying on the nutrients from your body. It's a way more equal world than it used to be, but men and women will never be the same. I expect Keith to do certain things because he is male, and when it's time to have a baby, he'll expect certain things from me.

You can ask your husband to curb his behavior to show respect for you. Keep in mind that he's not pregnant, and he will keep in mind that you are. Let him have his no-no food and drink sometimes, and he will be there for you far more willingly.

My wife and I are expecting a baby. I noticed that she started calling our unborn child the second baby. We never had another kid. It turned out she was referring to the dog as the first child. I think that's the nuttiest thing I ever heard. Is this normal?

It seems to be normal when it comes to dog owners, but you have to get her to stop that behavior immediately. I've been to many of these dog owners' houses, and these people are more into their dog than their child. They don't just act like they have Kid #1 and Kid #2. They're really labeling its priority, and the dog is #1. They have bigger parties to celebrate the dog than their own child, and their lives would be more devastated if their dog died than their own flesh and blood. Her behavior needs to be stopped immediately before she stops giving your new child (the real one) any attention at all, which I promise you will happen.

Start calling her by pet names—real pet names—like Scruffy and Bowser. When it's your day to cook, serve her some Puppy Chow. When she gets mad and gets dressed to go get some dinner outside, tell her that she looks almost as beautiful as Toto in *The Wizard of Oz*. If that doesn't sit well with her, then she might be able to understand why her behavior is not okay. If she loves the new way you're responding to her, get the fuck out. Too bad about the baby.

My baby is on its way. My wife and I are, naturally, talking about the roles that we will be playing once the child is born. She mentioned that we both need to change its diapers. I about dropped. I don't think that I should have to do that. I think it's so gross that I don't think I'll even be able to. Why would my wife insist on me doing this?

You're going to have to get over your fear. The same shit (pun intended) that you wipe off your ass is what you'll be wiping off your child's. This will not be the hardest thing you have to deal with after your child is born. Your wife will not always be able to be the one to change your kid. Man up!

Do you know the drama your child will have growing up in its own filth from the times that Mommy's not around? Even if you had a baby shit butler, there are going to be times when you're alone with the baby dump truck. Down a shot of vodka, and get down and dirty. There's no two ways about it—you're not getting out of cleaning number two.

My child is seven, and he's mentioning that two kids at school are harassing him every day on the playground. I have no idea what to do. What is the right action to take?

That sounds like second grade, which is too young to teach him a lesson about fighting back and that to truly stop bullies you must throw down a fist. You need to rock these kids' cradles yourself. Have you seen that movie *The Hand That Rocks the Cradle*? The new nanny, Rebecca De Mornay, takes care of the bully of the child she's watching over by going to school and forcefully pulling the bully aside. "I got a message for you, Roth," she tells him. "Leave Emma alone. Look at me. If you don't, I'm gonna rip your fucking head off." That's how it's done.

Tell your child that if he knows he's right, then he needs to hold his head up and not take any flack from the bully. Teach your child that bullies are looking for you to crumble, and that he has to stay strong. After the lesson, you go to the school and execute the plan that Keith just taught you. Never say a word to your child about what you did. He will think he beat a bully with his own self-esteem. He'll stand proud and not take guff from anyone again. Now put him in karate class, stat!

My daughter is twelve, and she wants to start dating. I can't decide if this is too early. She's a good kid, and I trust her, but I don't trust any guy wanting to be with her. Should I send her out thinking that she'll do the right thing?

Your daughter does not have to date just because she thinks she's ready. She has no idea what's out there. You do. You can say no. You have the authority. However, twelve is a very normal age for children to want to start going out with each other. If you're going to say yes but you're freaked about it (I certainly would be), tell her that she can see this person but only with adult supervision. He can come over for dinner, they can go to the movies with her aunt, and she can see him on group outings. They will still find a way to make out while no one is around, but you're doing the best you can. Make sure that she knows all about sex, the diseases that she can get, and that abortions hurt. Like a lot.

Like Chemda, I'd allow the boy my daughter liked to come over to my house or go to the movies chaperoned, but I wouldn't let my daughter date on her own until she was at least sixteen. And even then she'll have razor blades in her vagina until she's—God willing—thirty-five.

Another idea that I have for you (at no added cost) is that, before every date, you show your daughter video of a woman giving birth. Show her the agony and the tearing—the bloodier you can find the better. You can't overdo this. Along with the fact that since she was a child the wallpaper in her bedroom was made up of pictures of venereal diseases, she should be okay.

My son is thirteen years old and behaving differently from the other kids his age. He seems to have no interest in sports, parties, or any kind of interaction that is normal for his age. Should I be concerned about him turning into a hermit?

Should you be concerned that your boy will invent a new form of computer that allows him to rule the world?

Look at the way these nerds own everything now. That's the way it works. God only makes so many molds, and judging from the way you phrased the question, you're glossing over the parts that make him great: his intelligence, his thirst for knowledge, and his quest to build a photosynthesis bubonic hyper-chamber. So he misses out on parties and chicks now. That's not even his thing. Let him find himself, get his degree, buy out the entire town, marry the prom queen, and turn the football field into a new launch pad for a new fiberglass space shuttle. It's like social commentator Greg Giraldo once said: Do you think that if Bill Gates got laid in high school, there'd be a Microsoft? Of course not. He was into deep space chambers and I/O ratios, not baseball games and sneaking beer. That's okay.

Though social interaction is very important to a child's development, it does not mean that your child is a defect because he has different interests than the average kid his age. Take interest in what he's into. Ask him questions about how he spends his time. You'll find that he has more hobbies than you knew. Most hobbies have interactive group meetings. Take initiative to find out what they are and where they meet, and present the options to him. You'll probably end up seeming like the hero for it.

You won't be as cool as his *real* hero, Glodard from the Elvin Planet of Golgar, but he'll still think you're pretty neat.

My daughter just got her license, and now she wants to use my car. I think this is a dangerous idea. I believe that teenagers have very little regard for safety when they first take the wheel, and I don't want her getting into an accident. At the same time, I know she has to start driving at some point, so should I give up the keys?

When I got my license, I had no regard for anything in my way. I didn't think of the consequences that my parents and I would have to go through when I inevitably crashed their car.

Your daughter needs to have responsibilities given to her right away. Tell her that she has to pay for half of the insurance, half of the payment on the car, and all of the gas that she uses. While you're at it, show her how much responsibility goes into the aftermath of crashing the car, and tell her that she will be liable for the whole experience. With all of this, limit the time and distance where she can use the car. All of these things will not necessarily prevent her from slamming into something, but you will be limiting the possibility.

If she doesn't like the idea of paying half of the payments, tell her she can save up money and purchase her own car. If you want, you can buy her a cheap used car or an old one that you don't need anymore, and sell it to her in payments.

I was going through my son's jeans for laundry and I found a small amount of marijuana in his pocket. He's only fifteen years old. I had no idea that he was into drugs. I feel foolish and lost. Do I confront him about the weed or will that make things worse?

You don't want a son who's that young—if any age—to be smoking weed that came from God knows where. The weed could be laced with PCP or worse. That's why you buy weed from someone you trust, and you smoke that with him. You're keeping him safe, and you come off cooler than any warrior on *any* planet of elves.

Of course I'm joking. If what I just suggested sounded like a good idea, please turn in your parenting card. You're a fucking idiot.

Option two: Treat this like you would treat your son if you caught him with cigarettes, but, instead of having him smoke an entire carton of cancer sticks, make him eat all of his weed. Then make him eat all the grass from outside. You can say something like "Since you like grass so much . . ."

Wait, that's a idiotic idea, too.

Option three: Take the weed but don't tell him. Enjoy knowing how he's freaking out.

That's a silly one also.

Option four: Set up a hidden camera in his room, switch his weed with a bag of salvia, and post the hilarity you capture on video up on YouTube.

That's the serious answer.

First of all, this crime (and it is a crime) needs to be punished. Though drugs are possibly scarier than other troubles that your child has gotten into so far, you have to treat this like you would anything else he did that he wasn't supposed to do. Second, you have to have a very specific drug and alcohol talk with your child. He will roll his eyes and sigh, but he can hear you. Third, threaten a much bigger punishment than he's ever received if this happens again.

My daughter is eleven and wants a cell phone. Most of the kids her age have one, but I don't see why. I don't want her to feel like an outsider, but I need more reason to justify this purchase. What are your thoughts on this?

What you're thinking is that your child would have a phone and phone usage just like yours. There are so many options for cell phone plans nowadays. If you want to get your daughter a phone, you can have more control over it than you know. Most companies now have plans specifically for kids. They restrict calls to only the numbers that you allow, and they limit where and to whom your child's texts and pictures can go. The cell phone companies are on the parents' side because they want your business. Take the time to think about how you want your daughter to use her phone, and get her that plan.

Get her a phone, but set it up so she can only receive calls to and from you for safety reasons. Eleven years old and she needs to stay connected with the world? Like her life's so fuckin' important . . .

"But Daa-aaad! I need to talk to Julie about Paris!"

She's trying to trick you. She's not talking about a fifth-grade report on Paris, France. She's talking about what new endangered species Paris Hilton is walking around with in L.A.

No, she doesn't need a cell phone, and don't let her lie to you again. You look like a chump.

I am a father of a sixteen-year-old who does not seem interested in women at all. He started displaying a lot of effeminate behaviors, like grooming for too long and speaking more

flamboyantly. I'm not sure how I feel about this, but should I approach him about his sexual preference?

If he were straight, would you approach him? I don't know how many teenagers want their parents to approach them about their sexuality. The thing that you have to do—if you haven't already—is talk to him about the dangers of being sexually active. Even if you've already talked about it, bringing it up again doesn't hurt. This time around, make sure the talk includes all sexual orientations. If your son feels that you are okay with homosexuality, he will be more likely to be open with you. Don't push.

Chemda's right, of course. Your son needs to feel safe in order to share.

It's too late now, but maybe you should have played football with him when he was younger. "And the cat's in the cradle and the silver spoon . . ."

High/Low

People say that communication is key when it comes to any relationship. We agree. But it's amazing how much people *think* that they communicate when they don't really say anything at all. Friends, lovers, and family think that because someone has known them for a long period of time that knowing how they feel about things should be a given. The fact is that more than likely this is not the case. No one can read your mind. No one can always tell that your silence means that they've hurt your feelings. Certainly no one knows you enough for you to never again have to say how you feel.

Yes, as a couple, we can, sometimes, read each other's tiniest change in expressions. We know each other well enough to ask if there might be something on each other's mind. But this is not foolproof. Sometimes we miss things. Sometimes we misread things. That's why Keith and I promised each other that instead of pouting, being passive-aggressive, retaliating, or hinting, we would talk when something goes wrong, remembering that even though we're upset, everyone involved is coming from a good, healthy place.

In addition to the promise of open communication, we started a game called High/Low. We took the idea from the movie *The Story of Us* with Bruce Willis and Michelle Pfeiffer. Every night, whether we go to bed at the same time or not, we make sure we get together and tell each other the highlight and the lowlight of the day. Though we live together, work together, and could have done all of the socializing of the day together, we still play the game. It's amazing what you can learn about your partner through playing. Of course, like any game, you have to follow the rules. We made ours up, and you can modify yours to your liking. Below is the list of rules that we have accumulated over the years.

* Wait until the end of the day. It could be when the both of you go to bed, but it could also be when the first one of you turns in. The point is that you must wait until you can really assess all the day's happenings.

* Be honest. Don't say things like "My High was when I saw you walk through the door," unless you really mean it. If getting a new Xbox game in the mail that day was your High, then that's what it was. The exercise is to continually learn what makes each other tick. No tricks!

* We veto all obvious and "cop-out" Highs. For example, living with someone can't be a High. Saying your High is that you have the love of you partner is a cop-out. Obviously these are things that you don't want to take for granted, and you can say that stuff anyway, but the point is lost when every day you look at each other and say, "My High is when I saw you. My Low is when I didn't."

* You cannot get mad when the High is not about you or when the Low is. Your partner is trying to tell you something. If you stifle someone during this communication, they will not be as honest the next time. Wait a few seconds, think about what they

are saying, and then respond. Do not make them take back what they say, and do not be defensive.

We veto sex as a High. Sex is always a High. There is nothing better than sex.

After doing High/Low for a while, we, naturally, started adding more to the game. We began telling each other what competed with the Highs and Lows of the day. This led to more chatting about the previous twenty-four hours, and it helped us catch up with each other's lives in general.

We announced the game on Keith and The Girl, and we have gotten only positive responses from people who tried it. Some people play the game with their kids daily and have found that it gave them a tool to get their kids to talk more openly.

Try it, enjoy your enhanced relationship, and on behalf of Keith and myself: You're welcome.

What Did We Learn?

So, what did we learn? Well, if you're flipping to the last page of this book in the bookstore, then I guess nothing. Did you think this was all filler and we put the gem shit in the back? We cover some deep things with some surprisingly simple solutions, but it's still going to take you a little more work than flipping to the last page of a relationship book to get your love life on track. Good gravy. . . .

However, for the rest of us, who know you start a book with page one, we learned plenty. Right, baby?

That's right, Angel Dumpling.

Watch it, I'll fuck you right here.

But we did learn plenty. We learned the importance of communication, and we learned how to talk to our partners without being offensive or annoying. We learned tools that—even if the relationship you're in doesn't last—you can take with you to your next relationship. We learned that inner beauty is just as important as outer beauty, and vice versa, how to share your living environment with another person, how to date in the future with the Internet, how to deal with marriage, in-laws, and children, and, should you or your loved one misstep, how to deal with the aftermath of an untoward affair. That's a lot to learn while having a couple of laughs.

I think they get it. Besides, someone said something about fucking?

Okay then, Reader. There you have it. Keep this book handy to flip through when problems arise. Something just came up over here and I have to go. But don't forget to invite us to the wedding.

We won't show up, of course, because we don't know your family and friends and we'd feel awkward, but a wedding invitation is always appreciated. It shows you care. And that's really what this whole book is about.

Good luck.

Acknowledgments

Thanks go out to the *New York Times* bestselling author and friend Scott Sigler and our super-agent Byrd Leavell. Also special gratitude to our editor, Emily Timberlake, and everyone at Three Rivers Press. And, since we're talking, thanks also for various assistance from Michael Keller, Brother Love, Lauren Hennessy, Matthew E. Bray, Jerome Charles, and Keith McNally. Fuck it, thanks to everyone. Who gives a shit? Kyle Thompson changed the spacing on our book. Thanks, buddy. All our friends and some of our family supported us. Thanks to them. Why not? In fact, look under your chair. You get a thanks! You get a thanks!

About the Authors

Keith Malley and Chemda, the hosts of Keith and The Girl, are complex creatures that certainly can't be covered in a short blurb. They do, however, have thousands of shows—maybe *millions,* how would I know when you're reading this?—that will explain to you everything you'd like to know about them. Be sure to check out their free audio and video shows at **www.KATG.com**.